WHEN FAITH MEETS OPPORTUNITY:

Leaving, Learning, and Living in a Foreign Land

Y.M PALMER-CLARKE

 FriesenPress

Suite 300 - 990 Fort St
Victoria, BC, V8V 3K2
Canada

www.friesenpress.com

Copyright © 2019 by Y.M Palmer-Clarke
First Edition — 2019

Illustrated by Atrayee Basu

All rights reserved.

No part of this publication may be reproduced in any form, or by any means, electronic or mechanical, including photocopying, recording, or any information browsing, storage, or retrieval system, without permission in writing from FriesenPress.

ISBN
978-1-5255-5493-3 (Hardcover)
978-1-5255-5494-0 (Paperback)
978-1-5255-5495-7 (eBook)

1. BIOGRAPHY & AUTOBIOGRAPHY, PERSONAL MEMOIRS

Distributed to the trade by The Ingram Book Company

To. Hanna,

Hitherto hath the Lord helped [me]
(1. Samuel 7:12)

May you be inspired for greater

Olubada

Table of Contents

Prologue vii

Leaving 1

Learning 39

Living 121

A word of advice 163

Prologue

"A journey of a thousand miles," they say, "begins with a single step." That day, as I as I stood in line, waiting to cross the stage. I looked across the sea of faces thinking "this is it!" Finally, it was *the* day. It had been a long time coming, but my life, as I knew it, had changed. I was on the verge of realizing a lifelong dream. It was the end of a significant era in my life. I did it! It was finished!

As I stepped across the threshold, holding back the tears, everything else faded and froze in frame. My mind's eye wandered back to the day and ensuing years that changed my life and led me to be where I was that day. The steps I took had led me to this moment in time.

The LORD had said to Abram, "Go from your country, your people and your father's household to the land I will show you."
Genesis 12:1

Leaving: (v)

Going away from someone or something, for a short time or permanently.

1
The Wait

The journey, for me, started one September morning a few years ago. That morning, I awoke very early to the sweet sounds of birds flying overhead. Their joyously happy sounds filled the air.

It was a beautiful, sunny Monday morning. I had a lot on my mind and had not slept very well. As I arose from my fitful slumber, I sensed something joyous about the morning. In the distance, a doctor bird alighted on a branch of the guinep tree. Head bowed, it seemed to be picking away at something within its reach and among the leaves.

I could feel the heat rising from the earth. It was threatening to be one of those hot Jamaican days. The early-morning sun caressed the glistening blue waters of the ocean, forming a halo. The ensuing backdrop painted an idyllic picture. Looking on, I effortlessly embodied the serenity emanating from the breathtaking view from the back deck of our house. All was as calm as could be, and so was I.

A gentle wind silently passed over the land, bringing with it a whisper of the cool ocean breeze. In the distance, the trees swayed, making waves to and fro. There was a peace that enshrined the community. I had the feeling that something good was about to happen. I had been awaiting a special package for a long time. It could come any day, and I needed to be ready.

All was quiet and calm in the neighbourhood due to the absence of the sound of children going up and down the hill, frolicking and having fun while doing their chores. It was the first day of school and all the community children—dressed in their new uniforms and adornments—had left for school earlier in the morning. Many were being taught by my colleagues at school, who, unlike myself, were at work, ready for the new school term. Generally, I too would have been caught up in the excitement of the annual back-to-school events. This September, however, unlike these students and teachers, I was at home, awaiting my imminent departure.

I had applied to the Canadian embassy for a student visa in late June. It was September 5, and still there was no response. In faith, I had taken a leave of absence from my teaching job, believing that I would receive the much-coveted Canadian visa. I felt trapped in a maze and had no idea whether I was coming or going. I was at a standstill. I hoped the response would come soon.

I had received multiple emails from the college about the start of school. As a matter of fact, classes would begin September 6 the day after Labour day. I had been notified that I have a class the day after that. Luckily it was an evening class. If I were lucky, I would still be able to get there in time for class.

In anticipation of leaving soon, my bags were packed, and I was ready to go. Like Abraham, in the Bible, I was about to travel to a land unknown, and I was prepared to go. All I needed was the visa and permit to travel.

The prior evening, my mother and I had decided we would clean the yard and house on that day, as well as do laundry. And so, that Monday morning, we both started working on our chores. My father was a block away at his farm, tending the crops he had planted months before. At approximately ten o'clock, a white Toyota Hiace van pulled up to the gate. It bore the name of a well-known local courier company on the side in bold letters. As the driver pulled up along the entrance and came to a stop, I glanced up from my task briefly, rake in hand.

My mother, who was doing laundry, was closest to the gate. From where I stood, I saw her grab a piece of clothing lying at her feet. Wiping her hands, she quickly got up and approached the van to inquire of the driver whom he sought. The driver asked for me by name.

"I have a delivery for her," he stated, as he reached to the passenger seat for an envelope.

It looked like an official letter. My heart skipped a beat. I was excited yet apprehensive. I had been awaiting this delivery for weeks.

"Did you find us okay?" I asked.

"Yeah man! I have a few friends from the area," he replied, giving me the name of a known resident. "So, I know the area quite well."

"Yeah!"

"Please sign here," he said, as I approached the vehicle. I signed the white carbon receipt he gave me, barely noticing its contents. I was eager to rip into the envelope to unearth its hidden contents.

"Thank you," I said, as I watched him pull into the yard, reverse, and drive off in the direction from which he came. I rushed to the veranda, while ripping open the seal and edges of the envelope.

"Yes! Mummy, come and see. It's the visa! It's here!" I had finally received my letter of introduction to enter Canada!

"Nice," she said with her usual smile. "So, when you leaving?"

"As soon as possible!" I replied. "I am going to buy my ticket right now."

"Let me see it," she said, with hand outstretched.

I handed her the envelope that contained my passport and letter of introduction. She took her time studying the document.

Within an hour of receiving the package from the courier, who was long gone, I walked down the hill to the community library, which was located on the grounds of one of the neighbourhood churches. It has been there for several years and had recently gotten internet service. We were not yet connected to the internet at home, so I used the library's internet to search online for a ticket to travel to Canada as soon as possible.

There was an Air Canada flight available in the early afternoon of the next day. I seized the opportunity and booked the trip.

2
The Farewells

With much excitement, while trekking up the hill on my return home, I called my cousin to tell him the good news and to arrange transportation to the airport. He was at work, and answered after the second ring.

"Hi cous! Hold on," he said, putting me on hold. After a few minutes, he returned to the phone.

"Yes, cous," he rejoined the conversation. I could hardly contain my excitement.

"Hey, guess what?" I shouted gleefully.

"Hey! What's up?" replied the cheerful voice on the other end of the line.

"I got my visa!" I shouted in the receiver.

"Yeah!" He replied awkwardly. "That's good man! Congratulations!"

Hearing his sad tone broke my heart and spirit. I knew he was excited for me, but also saddened that I was about to move away to another country. We had been best friends all our lives. We were the same age and could be considered twins; we had been inseparable since elementary school.

"So, when you leaving?" he asked.

"Tomorrow morning," I stated. "My flight leaves at 1:55 p.m."

"So soon?" He inquired.

"Yes, classes begin tomorrow, so I need to leave ASAP," I said.

"Okay, I see," he said.

"Can you please take me to the airport?" I asked.

"Of course, I will!" He responded.

There was still so much to do; so much I would miss. Later that evening, I called a few of my closest friends and relatives to inform them of my departure. Many of my friends already knew of my pending study overseas. Before I had received the official letter, a few of them had helped me to pack my suitcases, and brought me items to help brave the cold. I had received jackets, toques, and socks. I asked myself, how does a Jamaican prepare for a place like Canada, and how did they know what gifts to get for me?

My mother called my brother to inform him of the day's proceedings. He and his wife lived in our parents' former house (the house in which we grew up) and they made the short trip up the hill to spend the evening and to wish me well. We chatted and laughed. My cousin, who lived a block away, also came by with her family for a farewell visit.

The reality of my departure dawned on me as the day and night progressed. For the first time, I felt the weight of my decision. I was used to travelling on a whim, but somehow this journey seemed different. The countenance of my parents, brother, and cousins did not help to lessen the load. I felt I was betraying my family by leaving them.

I had barely lived in this new house. It had only been two weeks since its completion. There was still so much to do here. My mind was abuzz with many thoughts, and so it remained for the next several hours. Somewhere in the wee hours of the morning I finally fell asleep. As I slept, it was as if I were sharing my bed with a band of wrestlers, as I battled with my thoughts.

Early the next morning, my mother and cousin helped me pack my bags into the car. Both were emotional and fighting back the tears. My brother had stopped by to offer support. As we packed the cases in the back of the car, my father looked on. He is a man of few words, but we understood that he wanted the best for his children; and if the best means I had to go, so be it. He seemed sad and withdrawn, yet he bravely smiled as we pulled away from the gate, me waving as the vehicle moved along. I was determined not to cry, and I did not, although I came close to tears as we drove away. This move was a step toward achieving my life's goal.

I was ready to wander into the unknown as I headed to the Canadian Prairies.

3
The Departure

My cousin and I had a tradition whenever I travelled. He was my official airport transport, and we always stopped for food along the way. On these trips, we would also talk and laugh along the journey. It was a time for catching up and bonding. That morning, however, proved to be different in so many ways. The impregnated silence in the car did not allow for any stops, nor much banter and conversation. Our attempts at lively chit-chat were futile as we both tried to grapple with the reality of the situation. I was leaving home, and my return was shrouded in uncertainty.

The drive, like the silence in the car, seemed to extend to eternity. We were each lost in our thoughts while also cherishing the moment. When we arrived at the airport, we quietly unloaded the car and rolled the luggage into the departure lounge. As I entered, I realized that already there was a queue of passengers, each waiting to be next to check in. In those days, there were no airport kiosks or bag drops. I had to wait for my turn in the queue to check in. I counted one step, two steps, three steps, four as gradually I moved up the line. When I arrived at the counter, I was exhausted from negotiating my racing thoughts and progression through the line.

"Passport please," said the clerk, with his hand outstretched. I handed him my passport and ticket.

"What's your final destination?" he asked, while flipping through the pages of the little blue book that gave me entry to multiple places.

"Saskatchewan," I replied.

"Where?" Perhaps he thought I was being facetious and was giving him a fictitious name. Luckily, my destination was visible on my ticket, which I had handed him earlier.

"Sas-kat-che-wan," I replied, emphasizing each syllable the best way I could.

"Where is that?" he asked, as he surveyed my passport and ticket.

"It is in Canada," I patiently replied.

"I have never heard of that place."

"Me neither."

"Sounds like it is far away."

"I do not know yet."

While all this was happening, my cousin stood quietly to the side, holding my bags.

"Please place your bags on the scale."

All checked in! We walked to the general area of the departure gates.

"I am going to miss you," my cousin said, with tears welling up in his eyes. "Do you have to go now?"

"Yes, I have to go. I will miss you too, but I will be back soon," I replied.

"No," he answered, "you will not."

What I did not know then was how the hand of fate would intervene, and change my life's trajectory. My intentions at the outset were to go abroad, study, and return to my homeland. But, lo, the plans we make and the realities that exist do not always go hand in hand.

After exchanging a parting embrace, I waved goodbye to my best friend and headed to the departure gate, where I underwent the regular airport screening and security checks. With full clearance, I moved to the departure waiting area where I waited two hours before boarding the aircraft destined for Toronto.

In the two hours wait before boarding and takeoff, I had many drifting thoughts. I remembered my mother, my grandmother, my grandaunt, my cousin, and the many relatives and friends that I was leaving behind. I thought about being so far away from home and how it would alter my life. I had plenty of practice being away from home. I had travelled extensively before this move. Perhaps that is why I was so calm. Deep down I knew, this time it was different.

Finally, it was time to board the aircraft. I stole one last look at the landscape of the island that I have known and loved since birth. At that point, there was no turning back.

I located my seat, 32A, on the aircraft, placed my purse below, at my feet, and for the first time set my carry-on in the overhead bin. I always avoided putting things overhead in planes. There was the persistent fear that stuff from above would fall on my head. I sat and immediately securely fastened my seat belt. I looked through the window, hoping to enjoy the island feel and view one last time before takeoff, before leaving.

I watched as the handlers loaded our luggage onto a conveyor belt and into the deep belly of the plane. The luggage moved slowly along the belt. A single bag wiggled its way off the belt and onto the ground. The handler grabbed it and tossed it into the cargo area. I wondered if I too was heading into the belly of the beast.

Preoccupied, I had not noticed that another passenger had joined me. As the plane taxied along the runway, I realized that a woman was sitting next to me. We quickly exchanged pleasantries. Then just as quickly, we each went back to our own thoughts. As she plugged her ears, I again turned to look through the window, thinking of all

I was leaving behind. The blistering heat from the tarmac caused me to squint as it reflected off the metal fabric of the aircraft. In the distance, I heard the flight attendant making the safety announcements: *Ladies and gentlemen, I'd like to direct your attention to the center aisle. We will be demonstrating our safety procedures …*

To my left, the landscape of my homeland was fading as the plane glided along the runway in preparation for takeoff, with which the distance became evident as the scene slowly faded and drifted out of range. The flight attendant's words became a distant echo and sometime during the takeoff, I dozed off. Funny, this always happens to me on flights. For every trip, at this exact moment, I fall asleep. The nearest things at that point seemed distant as my thoughts wandered off to things long ago, blended with things now and those things still to come. Foremost in my contemplations was who I was becoming. Looking back, zooming in, and contemplating the future.

Eyes closed, I looked back at my life to that point. My mind wandered back to my formative years, my mother, grandmother and grandaunt, who had all played pivotal roles in shaping my life into what it has become.

4
The Memories

Born in the 1970s in Islington, St. Mary, Jamaica, I am the first of two children born to my parents. During my early childhood years, my parents, my brother, and I lived in a large family house with our extended family members (my grandparents, uncles, aunts, and their families). This kind of family arrangement is common in my community and Jamaica.

When a child is born into a Jamaican family, the entire family takes responsibility for its upbringing. This familial arrangement allows members to share resources and take part in nurturing younger siblings and relations. It is also representative of our African heritage, as this tradition reflects the African proverb, "It takes a village to raise a child." In our home, managing the family and raising the children was a collective responsibility among the adults in the family, supervised by my paternal grandmother.

Jamaican parents are stringent, urging children from an early age to excel in their studies, even when they are not well educated. So, my brother and I grew up knowing that education was essential. We never missed school, even when resources were scarce. Our parents and extended family members taught us the value of schooling and discipline. My brother and I—as well as the numerous cousins that lived with us—were taught to value education and to work hard to become better versions of our parents.

I am the first member of my immediate family to have graduated from college and university, and one among a new generation of formally educated Jamaican women who have shattered the stereotype of being housewives, to surge ahead academically. I owe these ambitions and successes to my auntie, with whom I spent many of my growing-up years, along with the many other female influences that formed a part of my life when I was young.

My maternal grandmother emigrated to the United States in 1985, so I spent many vacations and weekends with my grandaunt, my mother's aunt, whom I called Auntie. Auntie's home was my second home. It could be deemed my primary residence, since I was there more often than I was at my mother's house. We spent countless hours talking about "the good old days," what things were like, and our family history. From my grandaunt, I learned that I came from a line of strong black women who stood behind their husbands and worked hard to maintain their families. These were women of pride and courage who had no formal education, but ran businesses and were role models in the community.

Auntie, like so many women in my family and Jamaica in its early years, did not complete her formal education, yet she was an example in the community, and encouraged me and other neighbourhood youth to strive for a better standard of life that could only come through education.

Looking back, I realize that Auntie's philosophy, though not often verbalized, extended to the many local children, whose academic pursuits she facilitated through her encouragement and sometimes economic support. Her home was a playground and inspiration for many in the community. There, I met many of my extended family and cousins whom I would not have met otherwise. She had a successful business as well as various farms in the district. I learned the value of education and hard work from her, as she insisted that we went to school and made sure we had everything needed for learning to take place.

My mother, on the other hand, completed her primary and secondary education successfully. She started her tertiary education at a college in Kingston. After her first year in college, family circumstances interrupted her studies. My mother might not have completed college, but she was a great motivator. She would walk me to the library to get books, and help me with my assignments to ensure that I completed them on time. We still joke about the time I returned home for a weekend from training college and my mother went through my bags and books to ensure that I had done all school assignments, and everything was "in order."

As I grew older and began to spend more time with Auntie, I saw less of my father. I recall him being a disciplinarian as well as a kind gentleman. With my mother, he ensured that we had all we needed for survival. Today, we have a special father-daughter bond. He was right there in the mix as I was shipped off earlier that day.

When Auntie died in 1994, I vowed to continue doing well at school and to pursue my academic dreams to the highest level, in her honour. Only days after her burial, I entered teacher-training college in Kingston. My sojourn overseas as a student was the culmination of work that Auntie and I had started, as she had encouraged me to pursue my dream of becoming a teacher. It also marked the beginning of my life and career as an academic scholar. Auntie left an indelible mark on my life.

My early childhood and elementary school years were fun and simple, yet they profoundly shaped who I am today. I recall attending Ms. Neil's Basic School, which was less than a block from my home. At this tender age, my life's mission had already started to take shape. I shone like a star in class activities. Well, not quite like a star! But there was conclusive evidence that I was destined for greatness. I was a high achiever and excelled in my academics, even back then. That little country school was my universe to conquer, and conquer it I did.

Even at that young age, I knew I would become a teacher and scholar. I loved school and everything about it. To me, back then, teachers were sages. Ms. Neil knew everything. As I advanced in age and began to teach students myself, I realized that teachers are smart, but in no way do we know everything. I recall explaining the little I had learned to anyone who would listen. When people did not want to hear, I instructed the trees, the grass dolls I plaited, or whatever inanimate object I could find. I mimicked my teachers perfectly, much to the amusement of my family members.

I am reserved, yet dedicated and hardworking. However, my reserved personality did not hinder me from being both a good student and a loyal friend and peer. And so, as I entered primary school, I had many friends with whom I played. My friends and I played many games on the hillside and beneath the gigantic tree in front of our school. The tree was a significant part of our history as students, because this was where we learned to spell, read, and recite our multiplication tables. "Two times two is four; two times three is six …" We sang those words as we took turns reciting our two times to twelve times table while our teachers looked, on wielding the rod of correction. One missed response and—whoops!

I was a disciplined child who loved to learn, and I heartily grasped the knowledge my teachers imparted. My quest for education and learning was earnest and pure. I became acquainted with the community and school libraries, and knew every book and section by name. Every crevice, every corner was my domain. I was reading above my grade level, ravaging my mother's many books and those I got from the local library. Like Marguerite in Maya Angelou's *I Know Why the Caged Bird Sings,* I often retreated into my world of reading, where I found solace and escape from the world around me.

By the time I entered high school, I was sure I wanted to become an educator. On the first day of class, I boldly stated that I wanted to be a teacher, unlike many of my classmates, who wanted to be doctors or flight attendants.

I attended an all-girl high school outside of my community, which required me to journey on a bus to school each day. Even with the long distance through Highgate and to Cromwelland, where my school was, and sometimes lack of resources, I had an insatiable desire to learn. My hunger for learning did not allow for absences. Therefore, I was always in the thick of things and ready to learn. Again, I soared academically, and annually my name was on the list of recipients on Awards Day.

As I progressed through high school, my natural leadership skills began to bud. I was appointed class prefect and group representative for many of my years at high school, and became a role model to the girls in my year and our junior students who followed.

After high school, I attended one of the few all-female teacher-training colleges in Kingston, where I majored in linguistics and Spanish. While at this training college, my abilities and quest for knowledge guided my path to success. I was appointed the leader of my cohort for two years, where I represented the affairs of my peers at management meetings.

After completing teacher training, I began my teaching career at a prominent high school in rural Jamaica. As an educator, I dedicated energy and time to my students and my job. I was always professional and courteous to my charges and the community. Because of my dedication, I gained favour and was appointed a teacher with responsibility shortly after joining the staff. It was unusual for someone to be promoted to such a rank in such short order, but I was loyal, hardworking, and detailed in my tasks.

I had earned a bachelor's and then a master's degree in education—specializing in teaching modern foreign languages—from one of the major local universities. While working as an educator, I also participated in professional courses to enhance my skills and broaden my knowledge surrounding my area of expertise. Thus, while engaged in my master's degree in 2007, I also participated in numerous short courses in teaching Spanish to English speakers. My quest took me from Salamanca, in Spain, to Mexico City, and back home to Jamaica. I wanted to do more, and so concurrently I completed courses in Public Relations and Spanish-English translation.

5
The Dream

Every successful adventure begins with a dream, and every dream with a dreamer. In the biblical story of Joseph, he had a dream from God. Not wanting to validate his vision, his brothers sold him into slavery, exiling him. Alas, their ill-conceived plot was a part of a greater design, as even in bondage, the young Joseph thrived. After enduring years of hardship and toil in Egypt, his dream became a reality. His vision became true when, as the second in command in Egypt, his brothers came bowing to him in their time of need during a period of great famine. Ultimately, Joseph reunited with his brothers and father.

In my case, the dream began when I was a young girl living in rural Jamaica. My goal was to become an educator with a doctorate. Like Joseph, I had many obstacles and oppositions, even from some unlikely sources, in my self-imposed Egypt. My determination had always been to accomplish my dreams and fulfill my destiny of becoming a scholar.

My love for learning and my dream to be highly qualified and marketable within my field propelled me to seek international academic opportunities. Moreover, I wanted to achieve a doctorate and become a world-class educator. The itching to accomplish my dream led to an earnest search for graduate programs in overseas institutions, but this time in Canada. Previously, I had focused my search on courses in the United States. I could find no suitable graduate school, so I abandoned my search temporarily.

So, the year I completed my master's degree, I realized if this dream were to become a reality, I had to do something. It was time for me to participate in more study activities. If I wanted to become a top professional with world-class credentials and be more marketable, I needed to seek world-class qualifications through study in a foreign institution. Furthermore, if I were to realize my dream of completing a doctoral degree and become a professor, I needed to get cracking. You see, I had a timeline that guided my career path. I needed to complete these studies before my fortieth birthday. I knew studying would be time-consuming and costly, and being single at the time, I needed to move on with my studies. This fact led to a dedicated search for a university that would satisfy my need to study in an uncrowded environment.

It took inspiration and encouragement from a friend for me to find my university of choice. After talking to my friend, I scrutinized the list of suggested Canadian universities. As I perused the pages of these universities, one university struck a chord with me. I examined the programs and courses that piqued my interest. This university's programs suited me well, so I applied and was accepted into my program of choice.

Once I gained acceptance into my university of choice, I scrutinized the then Citizenship and Immigration Canada (CIC, now IRCC) website to ascertain whether I was able to apply. To enter programs of study in Canadian post-secondary institutions, as an international student, I needed first to meet the requirements for eligibility prescribed by the IRCC. I was expected to have gained entrance into a Canadian post-secondary institution before applying for a student permit. I was also mandated to demonstrate my ability to support myself financially while studying in Canada for at least a year. The recommended sum was $10,000. That was a large sum of money, and it caused me great stress to come up with that amount. I depleted my savings and took out a loan from my local bank. Having met the criteria, I applied to the

Canadian High Commission in Jamaica for a student visa that would allow my entry into the country. The application process was long, with an even longer waiting period.

This dream, this journey, was as much for Auntie and my family as it was for me. It was my opportunity. This day my dream had come to fruition. After all, I was on board a flight to Canada to pursue my studies. It was well worth the wait. I was one step closer to the fulfilment of a promise I had made to my grandaunt when she passed in 1994. I vowed to continue doing well at school and to pursue my academic dreams to the highest level in her honour. This move was the culmination of work that Auntie and I had started, as she had encouraged me to pursue my dream of becoming a teacher. It also marked the beginning of my life and career as an academic scholar.

6
The Arrival

I must have slept deeply, because my next conscious moments were summoned by the voice of the captain's pre-landing announcement over the intercom system. The attendant's welcome message followed. As the aircraft entered its descent into the Toronto Pearson International Airport, I was excited, but also very tired. My mind was in overdrive. The calm I felt earlier had been replaced with nervous anxiety. I adjusted my seat to the upright position. Looking through the window on my left, I saw we were moving closer and closer to land. Distant objects began to take shape. The closer we came to landing, the clearer the images became. I had finally arrived. I was moving closer to the realization of my dream.

When we landed and were cleared to deplane, I gathered my bags from overhead and under the seat ahead of me. They remained as they were when I had tucked them away three-and-a-half hours earlier. Slowly, I followed the queue of passengers leaving the aircraft. Following the signs, I moved steadily toward the customs area, where I collected the two large suitcases which earlier had found themselves in the belly of the beast. These two bags contained all my worldly possessions at that point in my life.

I quickly cleared customs, but then had to negotiate immigration, which did not seem an easy feat. Looking at the lineup, I wondered if I would get to the front of the queue anytime soon. Not that the time mattered, because my connecting flight would not depart until ten o'clock the next morning. After standing in line for what seemed like hours, I finally was at the front of the queue. An officer checked my passport and letter and directed me to cubicle number twenty.

At number twenty, I underwent an interview with an immigration officer, which lasted approximately twenty minutes. During the meeting, the officer inquired about my purpose for coming to Canada, the funds and currency I had, where I would be living, and other general verification questions. Once he was satisfied, he turned to a page near the centre of my passport, affixed a stamp, and stapled my student visa. Handing me the passport, he said, "Welcome to Canada."

"Thank you!" I replied, smiling. My smile must have echoed my relief. This simple yet substantial document would allow me to legally pursue my studies in my institution of choice. I must guard this document carefully and do my best to complete these studies in a timely fashion.

I collected my passport and exited the immigration booth. As I left, I scouted the area for a place to rest overnight. The little funds I had would not allow me to treat myself to a hotel room that night. The airport lounge would have to suffice.

I spotted a café on the ground floor of the airport, which became my haven for the evening. I settled into the café lounge for the night, pulling two chairs together to make a bed. For my pillow, I used my carry-on bag. I propped my legs onto my suitcases. I tried to sleep, but I was restless, knowing I was in an airport lounge and thinking of the security of myself and luggage. The situation reminded me of another time and another journey. I was on my way to Salamanca, Spain, and had to sleep in the Heathrow Airport lounge as I waited in transit for my early morning flight. That was years earlier, and I had my best friend and colleague as company. On this night, I was travelling alone. Luckily for me, a few other people had decided to do likewise.

Finally, after many hours of air travel and an anxious, sleepless night in the Toronto Pearson airport lounge, I finally arrived at my destination. In true me-fashion, I hit the ground running. I was physically and mentally drained, but I was ready for my first day as an international student.

At first glance, the airport lounge seemed busy like the many others through which I have travelled. As my fellow travellers moved briskly to waiting cars and taxis that whisked them away to their final destinations, I followed suit, moving toward the exit sign.

With my two large suitcases, I was slightly hampered. I stopped to adjust the handbag I carried, which held my most valued and feminine accoutrements. By then, the weight from its contents was causing the straps to etch striped patterns into my tiny shoulders.

As I adjusted my bags, I took the time to study my surroundings. Narrowing my gaze on the people moving about, I noticed that amidst the group of people milling about, I was the only dark-skinned person. That was also true of the flight I had just disembarked. I had entered a whole new world.

I made my way to the arrival gate, where my friend Carlena would meet me. I had known her for several years back in Jamaica where we worked together as teachers. She had arrived a year earlier and was my liaison with the university. She lived outside the general area of the university, but had offered to pick me up at the airport and help in any way she could with my transition.

As I waited for Carlena to arrive, it dawned on me that I was in a town whose airport was characteristically smaller than any I had been in previously. The walk to the entrance was the shortest I had trekked. It seemed I had exited the plane in the parking lot. Standing on the corner, I questioned my location. "En qué pais estoy?" Where am I? Who would have thought I would be in this space and at this time?

I looked around, soaking in the view of my new environment. A quick look upward revealed the beautiful sun caressed by clear blue sky and lightly brushed with fluffy white clouds. The crisp air that gently sprayed over my arms and face by the passing wind did not escape my attention. There was a slight chill, which was quickly replaced by the heat of the afternoon sun.

In the distance, I saw Carlena arrive. As she approached, I awkwardly dragged my luggage closer to the vehicle. She pulled over, exited the car, and we exchanged a big embrace.

"Hey!" She greeted me with her usual smile.

"Hey! How are you?"

"Mi good! How are you? How was your flight?" She inquired.

"The flight was good. I slept most of the way," I replied. "I was tired, and I did not want to be bothered by the attendants offering me more water and salted pretzels.

"This is a small town, man! The airport is quite small," I said in observance of my new environment.

"Yes," she said, laughing. "Not at all like our airport in Jamaica."

"Yes, there was no hassle to get out. I just stepped out and there I was, outside."

"Yeah. Because you cleared customs and immigration in Toronto, it is pretty easy when you get here."

We quickly placed the luggage in the back of her red SUV.

"Ready?" She asked.

"Yeah! Let's go. I am tired, and I have a class tonight."

As we drove away from the airport parking lot, I wondered about my future. What mysteries await me here?

And so, my life as an international student began. I was on a mission, on a journey of self-fulfillment. I had joined the ranks of other distinguished individuals who have walked this road before me. I had no idea what lay ahead for me on this path I chose. I was a long way from home, but I entered my course of study with ambition, confidence, dedication, determination, independence, perseverance, and pride. I was ready to learn. *Bring it*, I thought. *I am ready.*

At the time, I had no idea how my diverse background would transform both the institution and me as a student and scholar. As an educator, I had a cornucopia of ideas and beliefs that could enhance conversations and practices. In retrospect, this is clear to me, but then it was blurred. It was unclear because of my need to fit into the new environment and become who I thought I was meant to be. It was not long before I realized that my ideas, culture, language, and beliefs could be integrated; I began encountering various challenges. No wonder so many students struggle to adjust, maintain, and attain successes in their programs of study in overseas institutions.

When I decided to take the step to study abroad, I had no idea what lay ahead for me academically, personally, and professionally. I had left the comforts of my home to become an overseas student. Entering a foreign post-secondary academic environment from a rich cultural, linguistic, and educational background, I was aware of the differences between here, my host environment, and there, my country of birth. Enmeshed in my experience and culture, I frequently grappled with my position in the university and its inherent nature. My approach to my studies and daily life contrasted starkly with the ways of the university. The day-to-day struggles threatened to consume me. I often felt like I was walking through the proverbial fire.

**Wisdom is the principal thing; therefore get wisdom:
and with all thy getting get understanding.
Proverbs 4: 7**

Learning: (v)
The process of gaining knowledge through studying.

7
The Unknown

When I first entered the university and my new environs, my thoughts and impressions were like those of a child in a new place. Everything seemed sparkling new, and I wanted to explore it all. In the back of my mind, like a mother's voice, I heard the cautionary tales of all the ills and thrills of being in this space.

As I ventured in, it dawned on me that I knew nothing about the community and its culture. This unfamiliarity caused me mental and emotional distress. My online research and readings did not prepare me for what I found here. I felt like all the lights were out, and I was groping in the dark for a switch that would bring light to everything. I realized that perhaps I was not as ready as I thought.

In the weeks and months following my arrival, I lived in curious anticipation as I learned the ropes of the place and people. Every move was preceded by a call for directions and suggestions from someone. It was a period of exploration, and like building with Lego pieces, I needed to unlock and interlock the parts to make sense of the new and emerging world I had entered.

Firstly, getting around was an activity plagued with challenges as I attempted to learn the art of riding the bus. Here buses travel "north and south," not "up and down" as was the common vernacular in Jamaica. Back home we paid fares when we entered a bus; here, I had to get a bus pass.

I was like Alice in Wonderland spiralling downward through the tunnel of uncertainty, being whisked through time and space, not able to fully capture or understand the happenings, clueless of the intricacies of my new surroundings. On that first day, I ended up taking the wrong bus and went around the city for almost one hour. That failed attempt allowed me to explore and learn areas of the town I would have never otherwise known existed.

As I moved about and conversed with people, I became more aware of the differences in dialects and registers, the different vocabulary and cultured variances that existed. When speaking with locals, the frequent mention of the words "*eh*" confused me. "That's awesome, eh! You just arrived, eh!" At first, I thought they were saying *hey* and noting to myself that *hay* is for horses. If this were true, why were they saying *hey* so often? Well, here I am, *eh*, still trying to figure it out, *eh*.

As I conversed and wrote assigned tasks, I was surprised that there were some words that I knew to be scholarly and have been using for years in the Caribbean and were accepted as scholarly were not recognized here, thus they were considered incorrect or inappropriate. Words like *postulate, posit, purport* were not used in the North American setting and I knew these to be legitimate words.

Further to our variant lexicon, orthographically, it was difficult to determine the correct spelling of common words. As I studied and wrote more, I realized that Canadian spelling was grounded both in American and European English. Still very grounded in its European roots, Canadian English has many words that adhere to the European style while others are American. The mix was frustrating at first since, depending on the professor I wrote for you I was asked to use either orthographic forms.

Depending on the crowd and circumstance, I also learned that there was a whole language system designed around a certain *f* word. This word played the role of punctuation and several parts of speech and tenses all in the same sentence. I often wished this word, and its many forms, were less frequently used. Its use often left my ears ringing as I tried to deafen my ears at its utterance.

The weather is a generator of conversations here. Of course, it would be! "It's nice out today, eh!" "It's gonna be warmer tomorrow." The weather patterns here are unique and varied, thereby making the topic a good conversation starter. Having the weather application on a handheld device helps drive the conversation, as one can monitor the changing conditions in real time. Regularly, individuals would have conversations about the weather while comparing notes and temperatures on their cell phones.

Checking the weather on hand-held cellular devices was new to me. Amazed, I watched as people engage in these discussions day after day. As I observed, I realized that it was not a bad idea to have minute-by-minute forecasts at hand. It was quite the trend, and so after my first winter, I was sold into the conversation. That winter, I keenly viewed the weather channel and would check the temperatures before venturing outside. Soon, I too was speaking the lingo: "Oh, today is bright and sunny. The temperature is only plus twenty-three. That's warm, eh? I would go to the cabin if I had one. This is the perfect weather for canoeing on the lake."

As they passionately discussed sports, it seemed there was an entirely different world of sports with its unique language; one that was only best understood by its constituents. "Did you see that hockey game last night, eh?"

Hockey, lacrosse, curling, and the likes were all strange words to me. I smiled when I heard the passionate talk of hockey. I had a secret joke. Hockey sounded very close to the Jamaican national fruit *ackee* which of course we eat, not play. Talking about ackee now has me salivating. I could devour a bowl of Jamaican ackee and saltfish this very minute. As for curling, my understanding of the term was apolar to what it means here. I thought of a heated comb that women use to straighten their hair immediately after it has been conditioned. Alas! Again, I was wrong. Here curling is a game of sweeping on ice! As a real island girl, nothing beats a game of football, the real one, and cricket. Now those are games that resonate with me.

I was shocked and I struggled with my differences when I entered the new learning academy. I was faced with the polarization of my culture of origin and the new culture. This divergence was evidenced through the opposing ways of doing and knowing. Amara, my good friend from India, was right about the difference in culture and expectations when she said, "you cannot expect to have the same lifestyle you had back home."

Similarly, in *Hunger of Memory*, Rodriguez told his story of being a young Mexican immigrant attending school for the first time in California. As a student, he quickly became aware of and was affected, even confused, by the differences between home and school. Rodriguez, however, understood that he must move between environments, his home and the classroom, which are cultural extremes, opposed. The opposing cultures caused the young Rodriguez to become quiet and withdrawn around teachers and other students. Likewise, I was conflicted with the move from my home culture to the host culture. The two seemed polarized, and often I made comparisons of the two cultures as I wondered about appropriate behaviours.

You see, I am from a culture and education system which maintained a hierarchical power structure and embodied a constant struggle for power between staff and students. In my culture, there are specific and rigid ways of addressing faculty as both parties seek to maintain this cultural stance. Coming into the new environment where there seemed to be a democratic structure, I was shocked at the relationships among faculty, staff, and students. Furthermore, I was expected to follow suit, and that perturbed me. I was surprised at the way students addressed faculty members. To me, this was strange because, in the culture from which I came, such informal relations would be considered discourteous.

Within my native culture, professors and lecturers are viewed as superior for having accomplished the task for which many students struggle. As such, they were not equal to students. Referring to faculty by their acclaimed titles is our way of showing respect. I have learned that professors here are more relaxed and allow for first name interactions to open themselves and students to the idea that together they are co-learners, as we both learn one from the other. It made teaching and learning less formal and allowed for the mutual and beneficial exchange of thoughts among professional scholars and "scholars to be."

And so, in one of my first classes as a student at the university I became encumbered when I encountered this issue. I needed to speak with the professor about the first assignment. Going up to him, I called him Dr. Xen. I was taken aback by the gentle invitation to call him by his first name. I found this difficult to do and explained to him that I would like to call him Dr. Xen until I became acclimatized to the idea, since in my culture this was the acceptable norm. It took me almost the entire term to get accustomed to this informal mode of the teacher-student relationship.

8
An Outsider

My first day at class was one etched in emotional turmoil. I felt neither nervous nor ecstatic, to be honest. I was somewhere between anxiety and excitement. I felt comfortable enough not to be petrified, and to accept whatever lies before me by way of teaching. I had arrived only two hours before the scheduled class time. Quickly, with Carlena's help, I stashed my belongings and returned to the campus for my first class.

I had conflicting feelings of excitement and nervousness as I approached the classroom. My countenance showed no evidence of my inner turmoil. Imprinted in my thoughts was the uneasy feeling I had of being in a foreign institution where nothing was familiar. I remember wondering: *What was I thinking?* I began questioning my position in the new academy. *What am I doing here? Do I belong here?*

As I entered the room, I looked around. There were about fourteen or fifteen other students seated in the classroom. The rectangular room had been stacked with enough chairs to hold twice the number of students as were present. The circular arrangement gave each student equal opportunity, as each face was visible. I spotted an empty chair close to the window at the back of the room. Not wanting to draw attention to myself, I quickly and quietly sat. Everyone looked up as I entered, eyes following me until I took my seat. As I sat, I placed my three-subject notebook, pen, and water bottle on the table. I was ready for class.

I was the last member to enter the class, and the professor immediately started her lesson once I settled. The first order of the afternoon was introductions. We were directed to talk about ourselves; where we are from, where we work, and the likes. I watched and waited as each student introduced him or herself. After a few minutes, it was my turn to talk about myself. During the process of the customary in-class introductions, it became clear to me that I was the "other" amidst the group. Everyone was from a nearby town or farm.

"I am from Jamaica (Jahmaykah)," I said as I introduced myself.

"When did you get here?" asked an older gentleman.

"This afternoon," I replied.

"Wow!"

"That's so brave!" remarked the woman sitting close to the door. "You must be very tired."

"Yes, I am, but the show must go on," I responded with a smile.

My Jamaican accent was pronounced and different compared to the other members of the group, who were predominantly Caucasian. They were astounded to hear that English is the official language spoken in Jamaica. Suddenly, I was representative of all Jamaicans and dark-skinned people. I was supposed to know everything and everyone black. The fact that I did not have this knowledge gave me relief from carrying the burden of being representative of people like me.

What was worse, I did not understand, nor could I react to the jokes and banters they so eloquently made across the room and within their groups. To me, they might as well have been speaking a secret code. This feeling was with me everywhere I went since my international student status positioned me differently from others who were native to the community. My cultural and linguistic background and social upbringing did not afford me many privileges when I entered the university. Additionally, my dark skin stood out among the sea of white bodies seated in the room. I was the black elephant in the room. If my accent was not evident, my skin tone spoke volumes of my difference and place in the classroom. The stares at first were of curiosity, which soon became fake knowledge of my origins.

The ignorance and curiosity were manifested on both sides. As the introductions progressed, I realized that although everyone in the room seemed white, they were not all white. I learned that at least two members of the class were Aboriginal, and one was Métis. To me, they all looked the same. In conversations later, I realized that many thought I was from somewhere in Eastern Africa. I had to explain then that I am Jamaican, and that Jamaica is located in the western world and the Americas. I am a westerner in every right as they were. A few were amazed at this fact. Others admitted defeat and surrendered. The line was clear. I was on the periphery, hoping to enter in.

I soon understood that on the premise of my international status, my experiences were characterized as foreign and lacking currency. I lacked the needed capital, which made it difficult to gain access to and enter the inner sanctum of local groups within the university. Therefore, I often felt like an isolate, an outsider, and lacked a sense of belonging.

The Oxford Online Dictionaries define an outsider as "a person who does not belong to a particular organization or profession." Being an outsider, I was not integrated into the group that I hoped to join. Within the concept of being an outsider is the idea that there is a bordering or a social order that determines who gets in and who stays out. The acclaimed Merleau-Ponty in his book *Phenomenology of Perception*, however, argued that "inside and outside are inseparable" since insiders need outsiders and vice versa for survival and, in the case of international students, to achieve success. Hence, I could not get on the inside without first being on the outside. Therefore, as the outsider, I was dependent on other students and vice versa.

The problem with being an outsider in my new community was that I was often engulfed in feelings of alienation and invisibility. As an outsider, I had the feeling of not belonging and of being different, of having a lost sense of self. Like the narrator in Ellison's *Invisible Man*, I wanted to be a part of the group and be involved and feel valued by other members of the group. The fact was, I did not fit in with the membership of local groups. And so, as I attended university functions and got involved in church and community activities, and I struggled with my position among the groups. I regularly reflected on life back home and the noticeable academic, social, and cultural differences that existed within the group and the surrounding community. I realized that I was standing beyond the lines of learning.

Researchers agree that outsiders in academia are sidelined based on the different repertoire of social, cultural, linguistic, and academic knowledge and skills that they bring to the academy. These differences do not afford such individuals full membership in the "in group." In my case, because I entered the Canadian post-secondary institution from a rich cultural, linguistic, and academic background, I was highly aware of the differences between "here" and "there," my country of origin. The way I approached my studies and daily life contrasted starkly with the direction of the university. These variations caused me to feel like I was living on the edge of my unique world and behind the lines of learning in the institution I had entered.

As I wrestled through these alienating feelings and encounters, I read the works of Victor Villanueva, Richard Rodriguez, and bell hooks. These individuals are scholars and writers of colour who also recorded detailed descriptions of their tenure as students in universities where they felt they were outsiders. As I read their stories, I saw myself reflected in their encounters.

I grew up in the days when children played outdoor games. I remember as a child playing the farmer in the dell. I hated that game. I hated it because in the end the "cheese" always stood alone. Why must the cheese stand alone? Entering the new academic community, I was unable to gain full membership, much like the "cheese" in the dell. And so, even as a registered full-time student in the university, I remained a "non-member" of the community, because I faced nuanced issues based on my background, which influenced my status.

I was always torn between there and here: my country of origin, Jamaica and Canada, my country of temporary residence. I wandered between the two because although I hoped to return to my homeland and reclaim my life after completion of my studies; I had to live and fit into Canadian culture and lifestyle.

My "Jamaicanness" dictates how I act in certain situations, how I learn, and how I appropriate myself within the learning institution. My ideas and ways of thinking and doing things never seemed to align with those of the new environment. These experiences and feelings reminded me of the work of bell hooks, who in her book *Talking Back*, wrote about the isolation and bewilderment she felt as she studied at a predominantly white US college. The element of her story that resonated with me most was that as a minority student she thought she did not fit into the university and classes she attended, but she was determined not to be a failure. I, too, understood that I was different and possessed diverse skills, and was determined to succeed.

Richard Rodriguez, in *Hunger of Memory*, told his story of a failed assimilation into mainstream schools in the United States. His failed efforts subjected Rodriguez to spend much of his youth in confusion, loneliness, fear, and depression. He was caught between two worlds;

neither of which he felt he fit into or belonged. Much like Rodriguez, I often tried to fit in with my classmates and the general community, but failed to do so adequately. The inability to gain membership caused me to feel like an observer, watching other people having fun and enjoying their lives. Admittedly, as I watched, some groups seemed challenging to penetrate.

That first day of class whirled by in a flash. The class was like nothing I had expected. First, everyone was surprised that I had just recently arrived and made it to class. Second, the course title was like none I had ever seen before. It was about decolonizing education.

Decolonizing, back then, was not a term that was commonly heard in the part of the world from which I came. Admittedly coming from a country once colonized by Europeans, I had to reengage my mind and all I knew or thought I knew. Listening to the other members of the class, I knew I was going to have to learn fast how to adjust. My mind was racing like Usain Bolt on the track; one hundred miles per hour as I tried to adjust to the different linguistic and socio-cultural nuances at play in the room and among the group. Furthermore, I had to be mindful of and manage my Jamaican English and accent, which were quite pronounced and bore its own nuanced meanings and intonations.

Sitting there, my mind flashed to the events of the movie *Forrest Gump*. In the movie, Forrest, the protagonist was portrayed as the consummate outsider. Forrest did not fit into any groups or career ventures throughout his life. Jenny was the love of his life since childhood. Forrest always tried to get on the inside with Jenny despite her refusals. He desperately needed to belong to her group of friends and community. In response, she often offered him a token friendship, but Forrest, based on his physical and mental limitations, never really fit in or felt he belonged. He always appeared to be different from the others. Although I was mentally and physically well, I often felt like Forrest as I stood on the sidelines trying to gain entrance into the group(s).

Often when attending social and academic gatherings, I felt like Meursault in Camus's *The Stranger*. Meursault, the protagonist, felt everyone else was "in" as they were *waving and exchanging greetings and talking as if they were in a club where people are glad to find themselves among others from the same world.* In like manner, that was how I viewed local students, faculty, and other staff, at least at first. I thought of their gatherings as an elite club into which I had yet to gain membership. I always felt a certain discomfort from the thought that I was not one of them, but an outsider, not a member of the group. The uneasy feeling that comes with being in a place where I did not belong always lingered. I did not recognize my alienation as such, because I am by nature very reserved. I felt the pangs of jealousy as I watched students converge in groups that seemingly shared a bond and membership that I did not see myself possessing. As I worked through this issue and sought a sense of belonging, the following words came to me. I captured and represented them poetically.

Outsider from Afar

They see me, yet they do not know me
Who am I?
I am an outsider from afar
I entered this haven
Now recognizing the ground is uneven
Will I be able to shine?
Will this place ever become my home, my haven?
As I sit and stare at their smiles portraying
An unconscious snare
Who is she and what name does she bear?
Why is she even here?
The outsider from a place way out there
By introduction on instruction
I keenly watched their reaction
Surprise perhaps even delight
This was no small plight she has the fight.
Minutes grew into hours and
Hours turned into days, months and
The feigned surprise every time I rise
Who am I?
I am the outsider from afar

9
Triple Learning

While pondering my experience and learning, it occurred to me I was engaging three levels of education. I coined the term *triple learning* to describe and explain the processes I negotiated as I sought to learn and become an accomplished scholar. Triple learning, as I view it, is a *lingua-cultural* and social phenomenon that provides valuable insight into how learning occurs among international students studying in universities. Operationally, lingua-culture refers to language culture. It has been so described because culture influences our perceptions and world views. Both language and culture play significant roles in who we are and how we speak and represent ourselves.

The idea of triple learning resonated with me when I realized that I often switched between three registers and sub-registers of English. The three language cultures negotiated were home, academic, and provincial lingua-cultures. Bakhtin maintained that students enter institutions of higher learning overseas with a repertoire of oral and written language that has characterized their thinking and learning. My home language and culture have shaped my thinking and behaviour. As I entered the university, I encountered the local language of the community, which is characteristically social and dialectal. In addition to my home language and the local community language, I also contended with the academic language used in the university.

Learning in a new culture was taxing on me because I had already internalized one set of cultural practices. I entered the university already ingrained with one style of learning, and so became unknowingly engaged in three distinct forms of education. This feature resulted in an interplay among my home, academic, and the local knowledge of the general community that surrounds the university. As I negotiated these lingua-cultures through my transactions, I arrived at consensual appropriations and behaviours.

As a student, I was often inundated with the sociolinguistic cultures that prevailed. My Jamaican culture was always struggling against the culture of the university and that of the environment surrounding the university, resulting in an interplay among my home knowledge, the academic understanding of the university, and the local knowledge of the general community that surrounds the university. If learning is to occur, the three realms are separate yet interconnected.

I entered my program of study from an English-speaking background and was accustomed to the use of an Academic English. Yet, in my writing, I often noticed that there were certain words and/or expressions to which I had become familiar that were never used among the members of the new academic community. My status as doctoral candidate positioned me in recognition that, like reality and truth, there are multiple "Englishes" spoken throughout the world and certainly in academia. The multiple variations of the English language are often regionalized and based in particular cultures so words and phrases used will differ according to the location into which we become settlers.

I learned through negotiation among three distinct registers of English. Fluent in my home language, I also lived in the social realms of the local environment. The regional, provincial English heard in everyday speech in the community is not the same as the academic language I was expected to master to succeed. Academic language is largely discipline-based and tends to be restrictive and more formal compared to the social language used in my home country and the local community.

This idea of operating in three languages and cultures still resonates with me, and I have evidenced it among the students I teach. Many students I currently teach are from China and have English as a second language (ESL). With my evident Jamaican accent, students are sometimes perturbed when I, the teacher, sound different from the recordings they have heard of other professors.

In the case of my Chinese students, I often observe them translating local and academic language through hand-held digital translators and cellular devices. I recall that even though I had come from an English background, I was attached to my native dialect, which I maintained with my counterparts and relatives from my homeland. I found that often I thought in my home dialect, and this transcribed into my speaking or writing. Fortunately for me, I have mastered the nuances of academic English and am often able to correct my errors. In the case of my students, many are still working on learning the language and rules and are often challenged.

Switching and translating from one register to the next points to the interconnectedness of the home, local community, and academic language in the process of learning. The three go hand-in-hand and must be properly negotiated. As I learned to switch appropriately among the three, a paradigm shift occurred that resulted in transformations of my life and perspectives.

Spot of light

In the darkness, I see
I see a glimpse, a spot of light
A speck, a tiny flicker
In a far distance
Zooming in on the light, maintaining focus
I begin to slowly move in to touch it.
It evades my grasp
As I move closer inward
The light seems to slither away, out of my grasp.
I slip, I fall. Oh no! I cry
With aching feet and a bruised ego, I crawl
The light always in focus.
Reaching deep inward I strengthen myself
I arise from the grime, brushing myself of all evidence of my fall
Some dirt eludes me, almost bringing down again.
In stark determination I move onward, the light is mine to conquer
It is to be my conquest
Determined I think, "I must reach that light!"
Moving forward through the cobwebs of fear, doubts and anxiety clutch me in their grasp
The light seems lost

Shaking, I part the cobwebs which cloud my vision.
I see the light is still in place
I shall continue to move closer, closer to the light as long
as it is in sight.

10
The Newness

I still think of my first assigned written task at the university. This seemingly simple task of writing a paper caused me high anxiety. In my previous studies when I wrote, it was in response to structured questions that outlined point for point what I needed to write and what my professor hoped to read. I soon learned that this was not the culture of the college of which I was a participant. Here, faculty encouraged free thought and critical thinking, and students were allowed to write about their interests.

Professors across campus seek to raise the critical awareness of students, therefore students can develop their ideas and craft appropriate responses that are unique to the individual. When individuals are critically aware, it promotes divergence in thinking and production, which makes for a diverse university and diminishes the power of egocentricity and allows thinkers to recognize that reasoning can always be improved.

I am a reserved individual. I never liked speaking publicly. I do it well when I must, but it is not my cup of tea. Usually, after class presentations, I would be applauded by my classmates and colleagues. "Thank you, Yolanda!" they would say. "That was good. A very informed presentation," they would commend me. "Your English is so good," a few of them would mutter. The tide had turned, because before coming to the university, I considered myself a good writer. I loved to write and could write on any topic, no problem. When I entered the university and certainly after my first writing task debacle, I became fearful of writing. I felt my ideas, words, and knowledge were not justifiable or worth sharing through this medium. My self-esteem took a huge blow.

You see, I thought I did an outstanding job on the written assignment I submitted. However, when I received feedback from my professor, my paper was decorated with track changes from the Microsoft application. There were questions surrounding the meanings of certain words and spelling. I was writing in a different register of academic language than the professor was accustomed. The negotiation of different English registers resulted in anguish that was bi-directional, because professors at times could not understand the meanings I wanted to convey through some of the words I used. On my part, my anguish was rooted in the knowledge that everything I thought I knew was being questioned and devalued.

Consequently, I often suffered from blockages that spanned days. I did not know what to write. I was reading so much. I enjoy reading, yet I felt like my mind was overloaded. Then, I would go to write, and I did not know where to begin. What should I write? How do I start writing? Is what I am thinking acceptable? These questions were my contemplation as I wrote academic papers.

In my previous studentship, when writing academic papers, there were strict rules and guidelines. The expectation was that articles were rigidly written academically in the third person; never using the first person. The thought was that academic writing should be neutral, and so, as the writer, I was expected to maintain distance by not getting personally involved. Therefore, the use of the first person in writing tasks was often highlighted and identified as inappropriate. It was very evident to me that the use of critical thought—self-guided, self-disciplined thinking with the intent of improving the quality of ideas on the part of students—was encouraged within the new university. Overall, there was a more relaxed atmosphere in the production of assigned coursework than I had encountered previously.

I remember a friend and fellow international student who became depressed because of the constant error correction on her assignments, and what she perceived it meant. She thought the changes were an attempt to prove her incompetent in the use of English. Moreover, she lamented that the changes made did not represent what she wanted to project. My friend became demotivated and disinterested in her responses to that course and assigned tasks.

Another friend and classmate of Asian descent was having issues with her academics and particularly in one course. She became overcome with anxiety because after toiling on a paper that she thought was to standard, it was returned to her with an appointment to see her professor. The professor was about to cite her for plagiarism; therefore she was not given a grade. The professor, however, allowed her to rework her paper.

My friend had no idea what she had done wrong and why it was wrong. She was unable to recognize how she had erred, since her culture allowed for and accepted the verbatim transcription of characters, based on their alphabetic system, which unlike western systems is made up of characters rather than letters. Having the academic capital, I was able to engage and explain to her what that meant. She subsequently redid the paper and got her grades reinstated.

11
The Stretching

It was not until I engaged the research and writing process while completing my dissertation that I genuinely understood learning by doing. Through this process, I got a practical lesson on this. My background as a teacher and scholar predisposed me to certain deep-rooted notions of schooling and the expectations of being a student. I thought I had mastered my roles of being both a teacher and a student. So, when I decided to engage in studies as an international student, I thought I was ready for the journey; after all, I had significant experiences as a student.

I had spent over a year reading and writing in the library. I spent so much time there that I was known by name by all the librarians, and we became friends.

"When will you take a break?" they often joked.

My response was always the same. "As soon as I am done writing this dissertation."

Secretly, I think they were becoming tired of my presence in the library and the many unshelved books I would leave on the tables after each day's use. Either that or they were concerned about my mental health.

Donald Murray, a noted journalist, author, and professor of English argued that writing is rewriting because it is in the process of writing and rewriting that one can articulate thoughts. As a process, writing is "not linear but recursive. There is not one process but many". I admit that I struggled with writing my dissertation. Every step was a challenge. Every word, every sentence, every paragraph of every page was a battle of words, wit, and vexing commas, which through sheer determination I overcame. I came to realize and understand Murray's statement to be true. The multiple drafts I wrote, the self-questioning and probes, and the realization that in many instances my representations through writing were unclear, frustrated me. Nonetheless, it was through that process that I was able to accomplish my writing goals.

I felt like a crab, stuck in my head and thoughts as I wrestled with and through the process; eyes bulging, ears popping, and my knees feebly shaking. People would come up to me with the best of intents and ask me how is it going, and my honest response was, "I do not know." I had no idea whether I was coming or going. I was spinning like a top and then standing still again.

I recently reconnected with a friend and colleague from my days at the university. We had a good laugh as she reminded me of how straggly I looked toward the end of my program. Those were the days I was on the verge of completion, but had no idea where I was.

She said, "I wondered how you did it! You were there before me, and I left you there." Little did she know my state of mind at that time.

Once, I was seated in the computer lab when a professor on her way to her office stopped in. She must have seen the confusion and struggle etched in my forehead.

"How is it going?" she asked.

"I do not know. I think I am stuck," I admitted.

"Okay," she said. "Take a break and come to my office. Let's have a chat. I think you need some perspective." I finished typing the last sentence I was working on, saved it, and went to her office.

"You know you often get stuck when you are closest to finishing. I think you have just a few paragraphs to go," she said. "You should take a break, and you will see that you are almost there."

"Thank you," I said. Surprisingly, that helped. Leaving the office, I felt a little lighter. I went back to writing and finished within a few days after that.

My state of mind was impacted by multiple factors. One factor over which I had no control always lingered. The availability of my committee members for review and feedback. This ever-troublesome issue had to be dealt with tactically. Bringing everyone together was always a challenge. With the busy schedules of the advisory board members, often there were long wait periods before receiving feedback. During those times, what could a girl do? I had to find other ways to engage my mind and to avoid going crazy. I would review the work multiple times, anticipating any queries or issues with the work I had submitted. And when all else failed to amuse me, I would settle in bed with a movie on my laptop.

Nonetheless, going through this process helped me realize that there are no texts that prescribe how learning occurs or how one is expected to act in the university. Individuals learn acceptable behaviours and protocols through interactions, engagement, and participation with other members of the community. It was through this back-and-forth process, going through the process step-by-step that I was able to understand. Then I was able to achieve a composite of the generic, transferrable skills required of and developed by academic study and research through situated learning. My ability and levels of critical thinking significantly improved through my participation in courses that needed critical analysis and deep thinking and writing. The classes I took required me to recognize, understand, and critically analyze in writing arguments I had read or heard.

As I wrote on a subject matter and learned to analyze arguments, I rediscovered how arguments were constructed, and became familiar with how experts in various disciplines think and communicate. I gained access to intra-disciplinary concepts, subject-specific vocabulary, and fundamental issues around complex arguments. This process is considerably more complicated than merely learning and repeating a set of facts. I was exposed to the sorts of higher-order thinking skills that prepared me to critique the world around me and I learned how to formulate solutions to complex problems.

Although limited by my culture and lack of capital, I was able to participate in the trade of learning through observations and participation in everyday activities. Notedly, through doing and redoing assigned tasks, I became more attuned to the protocols of the academy. While there were no direct attempts at teaching the rhetoric and academic rules for writing papers or doing assignments, I soon realized that this was an expectation of higher education. Over time, I found that through rewriting multiple documents and going back and forth with the write-up of a dissertation, I gained valuable academic literacy that would help me in my shift from student to scholar.

12
Nostalgia

Home, they say, is where the heart is. During this period of my life, it is safe to say I left my heart behind in my island tropical paradise, my home. As I penned these thoughts, I nostalgically reflected on the refrain of the song "Jamaica, Land of Beauty," scribed by A. L. Hendricks and L. Hall: "[f]rom riverside to mountains, from cane fields to the sea, our hearts salute Jamaica triumphant proud and free."

The decision to leave Jamaica to pursue studies in the Canadian Prairies was not an easy one. I was torn at leaving my family, friends, and home. Surrounded by the Caribbean Sea; the island of "One Love," Jamaica is home to more than 2.7 million people. Jamaica is from the Arawak word Xaymaca meaning "land of wood and water." It is the third-largest English-speaking island in the Caribbean. The diverse and picturesque flora and fauna that are characteristic of Jamaica form a beautiful and permanent backdrop to the island. Against this background, it is not uncommon to see palm trees swaying in rhythm caused by the crisp and refreshing wind from the magnificent body of water surrounding the island. The water coloured with varying shades of blue and green accentuates the picturesque scenery that one encounters on entering the island.

Harry Belafonte's melodic lyrics come to my contemplations as I too am proud to call Jamaica "my island in the sun." Known for its magnificent and pristine waterfalls and beaches, the island is also the home of Reggae and athletics. It is the home of the legends Robert Nesta Marley (Bob Marley) and the world's fastest man, Usain Bolt.

Jamaica boasts and enjoys a year-round tropical climate which on average registers high temperatures of approximately 26 °C and lows of 13 °C. The people of Jamaica are fun-loving, jovial, and kind. There is genuine love and care among Jamaicans, which is not only extended to relatives, neighbours, and friends, but to everyone we meet. So, coming to Canada, leaving Jamaica's natural warmth with no familial support, was like thrusting me into the abyss, into the cold. It was a lonely place to be. There was so much I missed about my home.

Food is an integral part of being Jamaican. Jamaican cuisine is known globally to be spicy. The taste of our island spices lingered on my palate. I longed for seasoning. I found the local offerings to be a little tame for my liking. My taste buds had to adapt as all of me did. When I first arrived here, everything tasted bland. During my first night, at the airport, I tried poutine. That was my first attempt at eating Canadian food. The person at the counter told me it was fries and gravy. Poutine seemed a weird word for food. I tried pronouncing it: *poteen, putiin.* Oh, I gave up! The taste did not quite resonate with me. What did I expect? I could hardly say the word, now this strange tasting food. To me, it tasted like it was pronounced. It was something I put in my mouth but did not enjoy much. Yet, for so many locals and visitors, it seemed an entreating novelty.

Because Jamaica enjoys a year-round tropical climate, we were never short of fresh fruits and vegetables. Growing up in a rural community, it was not unusual for everyone to have a home garden and a nearby farm. Thus, we had fresh herbs, foods, fruits and vegetables at our disposal. Moreover, if you did not have an item, you could effortlessly get it from a neighbour through their kindness or bartering. At that time, there was little or no representation of my culture and food here. A visit to the supermarket often saw me leaving with strange items I hoped would substitute for the authentic ingredients that were missing from the shelves.

Once, I bought sweet potatoes at the supermarket. It turned out that these watery tubers were nothing like the sweet potato I had grown up eating in the Caribbean. Here they are called yams. They bore no resemblance to the yams that we grew in our backyards or buy in the market on Saturday mornings in Jamaica. The sweet potatoes were not sweet. Also, they were as soft as porridge when cooked. My well-planned meal turned out to be a major flop, thanks to these water-filled look-alikes. I soon learned how to make do with what was available and grew accustomed to my new menu; albeit different from what I was used to.

I missed home and all the comforts it afforded me. Apart from our food and my friends and relatives, I yearned for the luxury of home. Here, I had to look for a place to live, and the houses differed significantly from the one I had recently built back home. I had to rent an apartment, the processes and arrangements of which were variant from back home.

Rogert's Place apartments available for rent

Bedrooms	Bathrooms	Square Feet	Rent
Studio	1	350 sqf	$849
1 Bedroom	1	601 sqf	$924 – 1124
2 Bedrooms	1	753 sqf	$1099 – 1199

Description

Information and Rental Rates are subject to change without notice

SUITE FEATURES

Each suite includes a fridge, stove, dishwasher and Internet. Some suites have an air-conditioning and a balcony or patio.

BUILDING AMENITIES

Rogert's Place is a clean, quiet and well maintained building that features on-site coined-laundry facilities located on the main floor of each building.

NEIGHBORHOOD AMENITIES

Rogert's Place is close to bus routes, schools, university, major supermarkets and all amenities.

GENERAL INFORMATION

Heat, water, and one outside energized parking stall are included in the rent. Extra outside parking is available for $30 per month per stall.

No pets prohibited.

Smoking Prohibited

It is hard to believe that because of a misunderstanding and lack of funds, I was almost rendered homeless when I first arrived. I quickly recovered and managed to arrange an apartment in one of the student residences. I had a roommate. I had not had a roommate in a very long time. Even worse was the fact that my roommate was a decade younger than I. She was from a different country and culture. We did not share a common interest, so there was hardly anything for us to talk about, save the affairs of the common areas of the apartment we shared. We managed to greet each other and have quick casual conversations, in passing, a few times in the hallway of our tiny apartment. It was a lonely experience. Often, she was away with friends.

I missed my relatives and friends. I did not have many callers. Therefore, a call from someone, anyone, was welcome at any time. These calls, however, were rare and left me feeling nostalgic. Oh, how I missed home!

Strangely, here you do not even know who your neighbour is. Everyone tends to their own life and family. During the warmer periods, they sit on their back decks, sipping wine and eating their various dishes prepared on big grills lit by propane. In winter, they lock themselves indoors, enjoying time with their family. On the contrary, all year round, people in Jamaica sit on their verandahs, looking out and greeting each other as they pass by.

My grandmother and my aunt were my lifelines. Their frequent "surprise" calls were encouraging and motivating. At the end of each conversation, I eagerly awaited the next call. Sadly, my aunt died in 2012, but my grandmother continued to call, and still does today, to "check up" on me. These calls were crucial to my psyche and academic success.

The lost connection to my family and friends, who were not in proximity, caused me to seek relationships with other students on campus. Unfortunately, there were not many international students from my country within my department at that time. I connected with the few I knew across campus, but I also made friends with other international students.

I must admit that the differences in culture and languages were obstacles I had to work hard to overcome. The fact is that friends from my home country, because of the similarity in culture and language, allowed me to freely and safely express my thoughts in my mother tongue without feeling different. At the heart of it all, I missed having my relatives and friends close. I missed being able to visit with friends and having them drop by unannounced for social visits. I missed those walks through my community, greeting and chatting with everyone. These days as I travel the city I am aware of the many faces that reflect mine. Over the years the numbers had grown, resulting in a more diverse body of students and residents.

Although I missed home and my friends, I found a lasting connection. After a year, I moved from the student dorm to share a nearby house with a fellow Jamaican. She had enrolled at the university a year after I had. This arrangement was more beneficial for me. My friend and I had known each other for a few years back home where we worked and studied together. Having her as a roommate gave the semblance of family. We were very close and shared ideas, household chores, and the likes.

Furthermore, in 2013, through the coaxing of this same friend, I met a man who changed the trajectory of my life. We became instant friends. Soon he became my chief motivator, prayer warrior, and partner. He was a tower of strength; a shoulder I often leaned on as the pressure mounted. Today this gentleman is my husband and best friend.

13
Failing

Back home I was admired and respected by my peers and community as a scholar, and my academic success made me a role model for many. My friends joked that I was a perpetual student, since there was never a point in my life that I was not engaged in some educational exploit. In Jamaica, I taught Spanish as a second language at both the secondary and post-secondary levels. I had also taken numerous courses abroad, but entering the Canadian academic setting, I never really felt like I was one of "them." I always thought I was missing something that would make me more like local students, and I felt out of place.

Moreover, as I worked and studied at the university, I never felt like my ideas carried the same weight as those of other students. Often, there were questions, stares, and snickers as I uttered ideas and concerns. Further, I had days where my knowledge was challenged by many who thought it useful to direct my every thought. Every utterance was often subtly altered by repeated statements in an accent familiar to the listener. They feigned misunderstanding and then would repeat what I said. To me this was condescending; mainly when it was clear that they understood, but just wanted to put me in my place.

On the day of my proposal defence, I was put through the wringer by a member of my committee who took issues with my topic and mode of investigation. As I entered the room, there were five committee members present; one joined us via Skype. For twenty minutes, I delivered my spiel confidently; everyone seemed happy. I talked about my position as an emerging researcher, my research interest, and how I hoped to conduct the intended study. I had spent months preparing for this meeting.

During the question and answer section, one committee member took issue with my topic and how I planned to do my research. While the member had no direct questions for me, she disregarded what I wanted to do and inserted what she thought I should do. Ignoring my ideas and explanations, she dominated the conversation, trying to persuade the committee and me that what I was doing was unwarranted and irrelevant. Treating my research and purposes like rubbish, this committee member argued and nitpicked every possible area of the proposal, while other committee members frantically tried to get her under control. So furious was the contender that at one point I lost focus. I suppose that was the intent, to put me down and to lift her up. It felt like I was in a boxing match and being dealt jab after jab, blow after blow. I was winded.

A chat with Peng, my Chinese friend, revealed he also felt invalidated and unrecognized by peers and faculty. Peng shared that he often felt uncomfortable and strange when his classmates remained quiet after his presentation. In relating this story to me, Peng admitted that he interpreted their silence to mean what he was saying was not of interest or value to his classmates.

The lack of validation was confirmed when he said he wished they said something during his presentation to "ease his pain." For Peng, recognition from his peers would mean that they saw him as a valued member of the group. It would lessen the feeling of loneliness and isolation on his part. An acknowledgment would also help him to "save face" which is essential to him as a Chinese scholar. To Peng, losing face—which is the image of self that the individual wishes the world to see—is a direct blow to his self-confidence.

Moreover, based on his culture, losing face or not being recognized is invalidation and is a signifier that he has failed in his attempt to fit in the group. Peng's perception that what he said was irrelevant was grounded in the "silence" upon his completion. He hoped someone would have said something to build his confidence and confirm that he knew what he was talking about and had shared valuable information.

To say the defence did not go well would be an understatement. It was disastrous. As the other members of the committee tried to rein in their colleague by explaining the process of my topic and methodology, the troublesome professor was adamant that it had to be done her way.

In the end, I failed the defence and had to rewrite the proposal so I could appease the committee in its entirety. I should have been crushed, but I was not one to give up. I shed a few tears after the ordeal, but went right back to work, picking up the broken pieces and reworking them into a masterpiece. Night and day, day and night I worked on preparing that document. In the end, and with much fuss, the professor conceded to her colleagues.

14
Finding Place

One evening while returning home from the movies, I had a brief yet frightening encounter. I had gone to the downtown cinema. As I negotiated a corner on the way to the nearest bus stop, two men appeared in my path.

"Do you have a quarter or a loonie?" asked one of the guys.

I could tell from his voice and the lingering odour that he was intoxicated. I glanced in the direction from which the sound came. I noticed that there were two of them. The area was dark. The bus stop was just a stone's throw away. I hastened my steps.

"Sorry, no, I do not have any money," I responded.

Not wanting to cause a kerfuffle, I continued without a word, which seemed to have infuriated my fellow pedestrians. My perceptions were founded in the shout from behind.

"This is our land. Go back to your country!"

The audacity of this statement made me snicker. *Who wants land?* I thought. *All I want is to complete my studies and move on with my life.* Little did he know that taking his land was the furthest thing from my mind. I was willing to share.

Funny that these exact words were uttered to me a second time, in the parking lot of a well-known supermarket. On the day in question, my husband and I were making a quick stop at the supermarket. As we got out of the car, we saw a group of men sitting at the side of the supermarket building.

As we moved toward the entrance, one of the men stepped forward and asked, "Do you have a toonie so I can buy something to eat?"

My husband replied, "We don't have any money on us, but we could get you the stuff you need from the store." This gesture was made from a pure heart. We thought we could add their groceries to our list while we shopped.

"No!" the man shouted. "This is our land!" This unwarranted response took us by surprise. What's with these people and land? Is that the most critical thing you can say to me? Feeling threatened, we quickly moved on to our supermarket duties. They were still seated on the bench when we departed the parking lot.

I felt judged and racialized by these members of the host community. In a conversation with Amara, she confided in me that she too always felt judged by locals. Professor Benedicta Egbo in her book *Teaching for Diversity in Canadian Schools* intimated that implied in the issue of racial discrimination or racism is the belief that one group is "intellectually, physically and culturally inferior" to the other. This idea is embedded in Amara's statement when she said, "you are judged on a different plane, especially if you are a minority student." I will admit that many times I felt like I had to work harder to prove myself, my value, and worth. It always seemed domestic students had life more manageable and were viewed differently.

I perceived that I was considered inferior to local students. Interestingly, the judgment and racism felt here was subtle, because there were no open attacks, but it was implicit in some of the comments and stares. I once heard someone said discrimination here was sugarcoated. The use of the phrase "sugarcoated" indicated a subtlety, and had me thinking whether I too had experienced this "coated" discrimination, or was this just a perception that we had about locals?

Once in the capacity of a group leader, I was planning an activity. After a meeting of the members, a few group members decided to have a meeting among themselves and make decisions without me. Only to report to me later that they had talked it over and decided to do the activity another way.

"Do you want me to talk to the teacher?" my classmate asked.

"Why would you do that?" I responded.

"To tell him what we have decided and to explain."

"Why would you do that?" I said. "I am right here. Talk to me." I listened to her and then responded.

"Well, that is not how we planned it. I wish you would have discussed this with the group before deciding to change the way will approach the assignment. And no, you do not need to talk to the teacher. I will talk to him myself."

In disbelief, she muttered, "Okay." She quickly moved away and soon was encircled by her group of friends. They stood huddled and spoke in hushed tones. I wondered what they were discussing. Maybe they were planning the next move in their game.

Peng once told me that he often felt "the scare in their eyes" when he approached people in the service sectors and tried to get help or have a conversation. The look in their eyes, he stated, frustrated him. He observed that individuals often went silent and seemed scared. It challenged him because he could not understand why, for example, an individual would be talking to someone and smiling, and when it was his turn they became all serious and business-like, and when he tried to converse with them, at times, they did not greet him, which made him feel insignificant.

Moreover, Peng had no idea what they were thinking and how they would react to him. Sometimes he said he sensed the fear in their eyes as if they thought he would suddenly turn and do something harmful to them. Sadly, he, like me, felt this way on campus most times.

Another of my friends told me that she felt invalidated in her classes and had to be firm with her colleagues. She noted that often in class activities, domestic students dominated the conversations and events to the point of completing tasks without her input, then would try to tag her on later. It infuriated her, and she firmly told tell her counterparts that she was quite capable of doing her work. They were very displeased and tried to explain, but she was adamant that she wanted to play her part in the process.

The thing with being an outsider in the university is that I had to work triply hard to maintain my status. It seems my efforts were futile, as I never seemed to fit in or find a sense of belonging.

15
The Struggles

A recent story on the CBC news highlighted the case of some international students in Sydney, Nova Scotia, who faced financial challenges. Unable to find part-time jobs, many of them turned to a soup kitchen for their daily meals. The story reminded me of my own experience, and the financial challenges I encountered. I can recall the many evenings I sat in class, nursing a bottle of water, intermittently sipping to keep my hunger at bay. Hoping to trick my stomach, I would take a sip, chew on it like a delicious meal and then swallow. When it became too much, I would visit the cafeteria in the basement where I bought a single slice of toast and strawberry jam.

I would take two or three jams and plaster the toast as I searched for a source of energy.

As I contemplate these varied experiences, the lyrics of Buju Banton's song "Not an Easy Road" comes to mind: *It is not an easy road, but who feels it knows… Lord help me sustain these blows. Obstacles in your way to overcome first* became my daily chant as I faced each new day. Mark Myrie, also known as Buju Banton, is a famous Jamaican Reggae artist who penned these words to record the struggles of the poor and oppressed. These words ring true to me of my time as an international student on my quest to becoming a scholar.

I knew that as an international student I would be expected to adhere to strict regulations. Deviating from said stipulations could jeopardize or terminate my tenure as a student within Canada. Many students, however, due to the practices and period of study, have issues gaining long-term substantive employment, thereby facing financial problems and constraints. I remember hearing of a case where some students worked more hours than permitted and met severe consequences before a local church came to their aid, explaining that they misinterpreted the rules. While I am not sure of the outcome of the case, it gave me much to consider regarding my status.

When I lived in Jamaica, I had a paid job and was able to accommodate my needs. I had a comfortable life and was able to afford most of the things I desired. In my new home, life was not that easy. With the limited funds I had, my spending was severely inhibited, and like Amara, I realized that I could not "live as I lived back home." I needed to be very frugal with my spending.

Upon entering the university, I received an entrance scholarship that helped significantly with funding my program during the initial stages. Alas, this was to be my only scholarship, as the opportunities for scholarships were few and far between. Available scholarships were very competitive and were awarded to more senior students, thereby causing significant lack on my part.

Having enough money was vital for me and to the successful pursuit of my academic goals. The issue of financial challenges is a global concern for international students, as most experience money troubles at some time or another in their student life abroad. Money played a significant part in the way I was able to traverse my study experience.

Not having the needed funds to meet my needs posed severe challenges that could have thwarted my study plans. As an international student, there was never sufficient funds and opportunities for funding. When I applied for my student visa, the embassy required me to show evidence that I could adequately meet my needs while living in the country for at least a year.

Here, everything had a cost, and without a job, it all seemed very expensive. Moreover, my tuition fees, like most international students, were significantly higher than those of local students, and increased annually. Upon entering the new academic environment, the lack of funds forced me to make many sacrifices in terms of how much I participated in social and educational life. Not having enough money limited my ability to attend conferences, since it required travelling to other cities. I often was unable to fund my way. Additionally, I would need a place to stay and other accommodations. I learned that every toonie, every loonie, every nickel, and every dime counted. If I was not smart, money could have been a significant issue that threatened my survival and sustenance.

My inability to work for the first little while hampered my financial status significantly. When I started at the university as an international student, I was not allowed to hold a job for the first six months. After this initial period, I could apply for an off-campus work permit, which would allow me to work up to 20 hours off campus. Additionally, upon finishing my studies, I could apply for an off-campus or post-graduate work permit within 90 days of completion. At the time, I was not allowed to work on my study permit while awaiting the decision on the application for a work permit. These regulations were revised and came into effect on June 1, 2014. With the new policies, students granted a study permit automatically receive a work permit that allows them to work up to twenty hours per week during the academic sessions and full-time during breaks, without being penalized or needing to apply for a separate permit. These new regulations also allow graduates to work with the study permit up to 90 days after completion, while they await the result of an application for a work permit. Such applicants may also continue to work on a previous work permit within these 90 days. Also, with the new policy, the student permit or visa becomes invalid 90 days after completion of studies, at which point the student is expected to leave the country.

Owing to the challenges I faced economically, I took various part-time jobs on campus to meet my financial needs and to survive. A conversation I had with Amara mirrored my situation. In speaking to me, she confessed that she entered her program hoping to get funding to cover her tuition costs. Unfortunately, for her, that did not occur, thereby forcing her to juggle many things to pay her fees. This work threatened her academic endeavours, as she had to work many hours per day and at times had very little time to complete her assigned academic tasks. What was worst in her case was that the jobs she could attain were time-consuming and physically challenging.

In my case, I was a research assistant, editor, and a call centre team member, each of which required substantive time at accomplishing my tasks. While these roles were rigorous, time-consuming activities, I counted my blessings, because fortunately, I never took work off campus. I knew of several other international students who took positions off campus which were even more gruelling and limited their ability to complete their courses on time.

Admittedly, my role as a call centre team member was not my first choice, but it paid the bills. I realized though that the nature of the job and the time associated with it were inhibitive and were impinging on my ability to complete my program in a timely fashion. At this point, I made the painful decision to quit, and concentrate on my study. The lack of a job resulted in a hard few months for me financially, but leaving that position gave me valuable time that I could dedicate to my studies, and I met my targeted deadline shy of two months.

Some days, I thought working and attending school concurrently was a double-edged sword. They provided the funds I needed to survive, while paradoxically limiting the time I had for studying and engaging in social and cultural or general activities outside of my studies.

16
Freezing Land

Prairie winters are brutally cold and harsh on the body and psyche of many individuals. Being cold is a strange feeling. One never knows what will happen when it is cold. Situations can change in an instant, without warning. Being in this kind of weather permeates one's entire being and leaves one feeling isolated. The cold is bearable for some yet for others it poses challenges and hurdles to cross.

Weather Alert

Warnings
3:29 PM CST Saturday 02 March 2019
Extreme Cold Warning in effect

A period of very cold wind chills is expected

An artcic ridge of high pressure continues to usher in frigid Artic air to much of the prairies. Overnight temperatures near minus 30c combined with light to moderate northerly winds will produce wind chill values of -40 to -45 tonight into Sunday morning. Wind chill values will moderate by early Sunday afternoon with day time heating.

Watch for cold related symptoms: shortness of breath, chest pain, muscle pain and weakness, numbness and colour change in fingers and toes.

Cover up. Frostbite can develop within minutes on exposed skin, especially with wind chill.

If it's too cold for you to stay outside, it's too cold for your pet to stay outside.

Please continue to monitor alerts and forecasts issued by Environment Canada.

I agree with Bonnie Byrne when she wrote, "I trust long-range weather forecasts about as much as I trust a politician's promise. At times, Environment Canada's seven-day forecasts tend to be as accurate as a coin toss and the Weather Network's 14-day forecasts are usually a joke." I think the day-to-day forecast is about as correct as guessing the number of stars in the sky. Experts seem unable to accurately predict what is to come.

Seeing the weather forecast above, I remember walking and falling one cold and snowy day. My roommate and I had set out on our usual walk to the nearby bus stop, heading for school. The morning was bitterly cold. With windchills, it was forecasted to be below -40 °C. As I opened the door to exit, there was a burst of cold air that lingered way too long for my comfort. In the brief moment that I had opened the door, enough cold had escaped indooors to make my face ache from its frigidity. The few steps from the front door to the street were covered in white fluffy snow.

Padded in heavy parkas hiding layer atop of layer of clothing, hoping to stay warm, we headed out to get the bus to campus. Heads held low, we walked along. Our steps were hindered owing to the multiple layers we wore. The wind was blowing southerly and was a direct hit to the face. Its blows hit hard and stung my eyes. I stopped to pull my scarf over my eyes. I needed to do this just right so the warm steam from my lips and nose would not cause a haze on my glasses, inhibiting my view.

As we walked, my feet were beginning to feel tingly. Bravely, I continued on my journey. Dragging myself through the thick snow, plodding along, I felt my feet going numb. Before I realized what had happened, I found myself slipping to the ground. Down I went with one thud. The cold air had slowly crept in through my pants, long johns, and socks to numb every nerve in my tiny legs, resulting in my fall on the snowy, icy road.

My friend, who was a little ahead, heard my fall and ran to my side. A passing vehicle stopped. Its occupant, a kind lady, inquired whether I was well.

"I am good, thank you," I replied as I slowly and awkwardly, with the help of my friend, rose from where my lifeless legs had so effortlessly placed me moments earlier. It was my first real fall in Canada, and I can still remember the shivers that ran down my spine to my legs as I tried to stand and regain my composure. It felt like someone was jolting electricity into my veins, which were fighting vigorously to withstand. Standing firm again required me to mentally fight the excessive compulsion of my almost frozen feet to buckle under the weight. I was not heavy-set, but the ice in my thin legs was, and it threatened to carry me under once more. It took considerable effort to lift myself and carry on with my day.

Of course, I had challenges adapting to colder weather. I still do. In Jamaica, I was the one most likely to be clad in sweaters all day in the scorching sun, claiming to be cold. Therefore, the shift to these cold temperatures caused me much agitation and distress as I tried to adjust to my new environment.

Coming from a warm country, I had no idea what "minus" temperatures meant. My only knowledge of freezing temperatures was from the freezers we kept at home for ice and frozen drinks. Even then our freezers seem to be heat-boxes compared to the cold we feel here. Yes, I did my research. I read the numbers and all that. Nonetheless, I could never imagine what it would feel like living in and experiencing negative temperatures. It is not until I experienced the first winter that I realized. Even then, I could not fathom its depth. It was then that I wondered where I was and what had gotten myself into.

Never had I suffered such bone-chilling cold, nor was I accustomed to seeing and feeling the white fluffy snow that forms part of the Canadian physical landscape. As I permeated the path to scholarship, I struggled with the shifting temperatures and especially with the extremely low temperatures during the winter period. The reality of the weather condition could have caused me to spiral into any number of psychological disorders.

I learned there was a disorder called seasonal affective disorder (SAD). Who knew that there was such a thing? It was not until I entered university in Canada that I learned of its existence from a friend. The Canadian Mental Health Association (CMHA) defines SAD as a type of depression that occurs in individuals at certain times of the year. Typically, SAD begins to surface during fall and lasts through the winter. While this is the most common period, SAD also affects people in the summer. Summer's SAD begins in spring and continues through the summer months. There are no confirmed causes of SAD. Well, truth be told I do not like SAD nor did I want to have SAD. This disease had the potential of thwarting my academic goals. Avoiding this plague is quite a feat, I admit. I have heard people describe the weather condition as "harsh," "bad," "tough," and "boring," and shared stories of feeling alienated and lost, especially during the dark, dreary days of winter. Amara swears it has the potential to "slow you down."

When I first arrived in this, the city it was fall. That year, the first snowfall was early October. I looked through my window and envisaged going out in such conditions. In my head, I had a conversation fully ratifying why I should not go outside. As a Jamaican I had never seen snow. My thinking was, *Look outside. There is so much snow on the ground; how do I walk in so much snow? No one will be outdoors in this weather.* I decided not to go out that day. Instead, I viewed the snow from the window while entangled in a sea of nostalgia, drifting along with the gentle island breeze, my skin kissed by the tropical sun. Embedded in my self-deliberations were feelings of confusion and alienation. As I looked out in the distance, I saw an elderly lady wading through the snow. She seemed comfortable enough. I viewed all this in dismay, thinking, if she could do it so should I. Moreover, I am here for school and will need to go out at some point.

The next Monday morning I was up sooner than the cock could crow. I had arisen early that day because it would be my first time going out into the snow (the *S* word I call it). What was more, I had an 8:30 a.m. class. Getting dressed was no easy feat, considering the multiple layers I had to manoeuvre. Clad in blue jeans with long johns snuggly hugging my legs beneath, I covered my upper body with a pink sweater I had gotten from my friend back home, but not before putting on two layers underneath. The lower half of my body was complete with two pairs of socks and my Walmart sourced winter boots. To complete my ensemble, I covered myself with the ten-pound jacket I had bought at Value Village on my friend's insistence. As I stepped out that morning, I was heavy and ready for war.

Fast-forward seven and a half years later, this year, the cold was overbearing. As I write, the temperature is -37 °C. Can you believe it? Thirty-seven below is colder than any freezer known to man! At one point during this winter, I lived in the coldest place on earth. I am surprised that my organs still work. Trekking across mountains of snow high enough to bury me for eternity. I keep surviving in these frozen lands.

Freezing Land

I am from a land of sun, sea, and sand
These are the treasures of my native land.
Time like the sand rushes through our fingers
We are unable to grasp it never lingers
Here frozen like the willows, I gasp and shiver at this ghastly coldness
    Grasping and lugging at my body from vice grips of ice
        No man this is nice!
        Back home people sipping drinks with ice
        Here I am walking, slipping and swaying on ice.
    I depend on my inner voice to help me to make the right choice
As I struggle with the thought of warmth and the reality of this iciness
        Come reason with me.
Why did I leave my sweet country of sun, sand, and sea to dwell here in these frozen lands?
        They giggle, and they ask
        Liking it here yet?
        What? Like it here?
Me, a stranger, a nomad, an outcast still living in this frozen land.

17
The Mentoring

Although I spent most of my time in my head trying to figure things out, I had great mentors. Generally, the terms mentor and mentee describe a relationship between professor/advisor/research supervisor and student. During my study, I learned from students and professors. My attendance and participation in group discussions and activities allowed me to be mentored by other students as well. These fellow students were more familiar with the ways of academic literacy and modelled for me through writing thoughtful papers and doing high quality oral presentations.

Apart from observing and imitating local students, two women supported and mentored me through the process.

I met them both during my first year at university. They reminded me of two brilliant professors at the University of the West Indies, Jamaica, who had taken me under their wings and moulded my professional and academic skills. They had laid the groundwork well because when I met these women in my Canadian university, I was ready. I was prepared both to work and be groomed into the next phase of my academic path. Both were staunchly different in their world views and outlook, and together they enriched my experience.

I met Karla when I first started my program of study. She was one of the first professors I met when I arrived. She was jovial and kind. She too had come to Canada from another region. She had walked the walk and excelled in academia. Her views were different and intriguing, based on her Indigenous traditions. We met in her office on a Wednesday afternoon to discuss my candidacy and her availability to supervise my doctoral work. We talked at length about my life, where I am from, and my research interests. We chatted for about an hour. She decided that she would supervise my doctoral work. She seemed genuinely excited about working with me, and more so, about my topic.

As we talked, she looked me squarely in the eyes and said, "Look at both of us. Do you see who we are? We are two brown-skinned people. We have a lot of work ahead of us!"

And so there was.

The second woman, Linda, I first met in February of 2012. I visited her at her office to discuss my doctoral research and to learn about her availability to work with me in the process. Her office was located on the third floor of the department building. She was a busy professor who was hard to pin down, yet I managed to make an appointment with her for 10:00 a.m. that Tuesday morning. We were to discuss my program and path to a PhD. I was at her office door at 9:50 am. When I knocked on her door, there a was a pleasant "Hello! Come in." Her warm welcome made me feel at home and at peace.

She was pleasant, calm, and very reassuring as I sat across from her and detailed what I intended to do. Instantly, she became my mentor and friend. In fact, we are still very close today. Straightaway, I perceived the differences in the professor-student relationship. She was approachable and sought to assist me with adaptation strategies and the planning and implementation of my academic path.

My mentors not only catered to my academic desires, but they were also like family. I had found a home away from home. These professor-student relationships positioned me as being of significance and helped me to integrate into the group as a *scholar-to-be* and *faculty-in-waiting*. Through these relationships, I had valid contacts within the university and was able to have conversations and discussions with them not only as mentors, but also as colleagues. These conversations helped to put my mind at ease and gave me a comfort level through which I could dedicate more effort to my studies.

My mentors became like my mothers. We had regular social gatherings where I would talk about my work. They also introduced me to numerous colleagues and they boasted of my work and development. One faculty was very keen on what I was doing and became a mentor in her own right. Susan is a spunky professor. She is an advocate for social change and inequities. We have had many conversations about my experience. We still maintain contact to date.

This experience of professor-student relationship reiterated my need for belonging and relationships. Also evident was the power of this relationship and how it enabled me to improve my scholarship. Through these relationships, I felt valued and vital to the processes of learning and culture within the university. Having this sense of belonging enabled and motivated me to engage more fully in my studies, thereby leading to the successful completion of my course.

Have not I commanded thee? Be strong and of a good courage; be not afraid, neither be thou dismayed: for the LORD thy God is with thee whithersoever thou goest.
Joshua 1:9 (KJV)

Living: (v)

To have a home; to dwell; to reside

Becoming

Thinking back, way back and I am in shock!
The barefooted tyke who
Ran the streets gleefully frolicking.
Stones clicking, birds chirping, rivers flowing. This girl
is becoming
Like nature's cocooned innocence, her light is
being unwrapped
Suddenly she bursts into recognition.
Recognition that she can be all she can be.
She is becoming.
Mountains and plains
Near and far
Melting, merging into one this shy island girl
is becoming
She is becoming who God wants her to be
In stages, never fazing
She continues to become.

18
The Transformation

Funny how we get excited by the prospect of living and studying overseas. It seems simple enough to shift from one environment to the next. I too thought this transition would be smooth. My goal has always been to earn a doctorate and become a professor and scholar. The trajectory to meeting this desire was not always clear, yet my goal was still in sight. I thought because I was an educator and had travelled, I had the requisite skills to integrate into my new university and community seamlessly.

When I arrived in Canada, it was immediately clear to me that this was not an easy switch. The minute I disembarked my flight at my destination, I pondered my future and wondered how I would make do in this new land.

How would I successfully traverse the path I had chosen? Entering the Canadian postsecondary environment from a rich cultural, linguistic, and educational background, I was highly aware of the differences between *here*, my host environment, and *there*, my country of birth.

I had left my home country with all the privileges it provided me to enter an unfamiliar postsecondary climate; a setting in which I was a stranger, outsider, social isolate, and an individual devoid of the necessary capital to make my presence count. I often felt isolated because I lacked the dominant economic, cultural, and social capital required to survive within the new host community.

Through my journey and research, I found the path from student to scholar to be holistic, experiential, and transformational. I left my home, ambitious and fully intent on becoming a better human being; that is, on achieving self-actualization through my studies. My choice of university and research was based on my need to be better, to "become." I was often challenged by variances in the linguistic and social culture of the new community and environment.

So, there I was, a student, a scholar-to-be who had entered the university with different knowledge and skills. I was amply qualified for the level of study in which I chose to engage, having studied previously at the tertiary level in my home country. I had a master's degree in education and had entered graduate studies after working as a teacher for more than fifteen years. I had given valuable service and contributed to my community of origin. I aimed to become accomplished in my field of study and gain mastery that would allow me to act independently. The acquisition of *master* status, I thought, would position me as a scholar; no longer would I be a scholar-to-be or a scholar-in-waiting. Instead, through my daily work in the academy, I was able to acquire the requisite scholarly knowledge of conversation, mindful reading, and written discourse, as well as the ability to think and analyze critically.

I entered one department, and by the end of the first semester, I was looking to transfer to another. My transfer had nothing to do with a deficiency within the current department, but that the offerings of the new department better fit my ambitions. I would be able to accomplish my goal of attaining a Doctor of Philosophy degree, allowing me to become the scholar I hoped to become.

Aristotle argued that the term *being* usually presupposed the idea of becoming, which means that one must be at a particular state before one can become another. I was always shifting roles as I searched for meaning, and negotiating ethical behaviours owing to my outsider status and inherent lack of the requisite social, cultural, academic, and linguistic capital. In essence, I became who I needed to be; much like a figured being; as a means of surviving in the host community. I then had to step out of my comfort zone to confront new and varied situations.

Unbeknownst to me, my worldview was gradually transforming as I was becoming "better" through my social, cultural, and academic encounters. Therefore, as I traversed the university and negotiated the many challenges I faced, I was moving from being a dependent student to becoming an independent scholar. Admittedly, the seemingly negative realities of my experience consumed my thoughts, thereby hindering my ability to appreciate the subtle yet very potent changes that were occurring within me.

I realized that while I could not adequately express and detail the shifts and turns in my thinking, I was actively engaged in the process of transformation from student to scholar. The internal and external maneuvers in which I was engrossed daily were responsible for my conversion. This reality was not immediately apparent as I expended my energies on adapting to the new academic and social setting and negotiating my daily tasks. I was oblivious to the changes as they happened. It was not until I sat to think it through as I wrote this book that I understood that a shift had occurred. Admittedly, I was almost swept away with my perceptions of my experiences, which prevented me from seeing reality. I had not realized the path of transformation. I almost missed that I was becoming.

19
The Return Home

On a trip home in 2013, I realized that I was not the same as before I left. Something had changed. I had changed.

I disembarked my flight in Montego Bay, Jamaica. As I exited the airport, the Jamaican sun greeted me with blistering heat. I dragged my bags to the waiting area at the arrival gate. My cousin had not yet arrived. As I waited, a gentleman approached me to ask whether I needed a taxi.

"No man mi good," I replied, "but you can lend me your phone."

"Yeah man, dat not a problem man," he said. I watched as he reached into his rear pants pocket, removed and handed me his phone. It was a simple phone. "Bangers" they are called in Jamaica. His banger phone was good enough to make the call. That is all I needed. I dialled my cousin's number to alert him that my flight had arrived. He was just around the corner in the nearby waiting bay. I hung up thanked my new friend and returned his phone. "No problem man," he responded. While I turned my attention to my luggage and the arrival of my ride, my gentleman friend remained by my side. He seemed to be in the mood for a conversation. I was too tired to engage in one. All I wanted was to be on my way.

As I looked up, I saw my cousin's car approaching. Quickly we stacked the bags in the trunk of the vehicle, and we were off, but not before we greeted each other with a hug. As we drove away, I looked around at the landscape. Things were different. The many new structures that lined the once vacant lots told of the many changes that occurred.

This time, there was no awkwardness as my cousin and I chatted and laughed about our days growing up. We caught up with each other's life. I talked about my time abroad to date, and he told me about his family, and all the new developments that had occurred in the country and our community. I saw evidence of many of his stories as we drove past new businesses and hotels along the coastline.

I wanted to surprise my mother, so I asked my cousin to stop at a supermarket in the capital city. I was going to get her groceries. Walking through the supermarket aisles was a strange encounter. I observed every aisle and tried to make a comparison in price and nature in my brain. As I started to fill the shopping cart, I noticed the prices. Whoa, wow! Everything seemed so expensive! I had an instant headache. I decided I could not complete this task. I will have my mother do her shopping. Moreover, only she knew what she needed.

I began sensing the change in me then. It seemed so much had changed in such a short time. The vibrant Jamaican language did not fail me, even though the slangs and expressions had evolved. The places seemed different; people looked and sounded different. I was different. My perspectives had changed.

When I arrived at my mother's house, my cousin and I decided to play a prank on her. He told me to stay in the car while he proceeded to get my mother with the ruse of her helping him to get something from the car. As she approached the vehicle, I shrank back in the rear seat, stifling a laugh. She came around to the side and opened the door. When she saw me sitting there, she started laughing. You could see the joy in her eyes as they lit up.

"Mi did know say a somebody in a di car enuh" (I knew there was someone in the car.)

"How yuh know?" (How did you know) asked my cousin, laughing.

"Is alright," (It's ok) she said as she hugged and kissed me.

"Suh yuh cudn tell me yuh cumin?" (Why didn't you tell me you were coming?)

"It was to be a surprise," I answered, smiling.

"Mi mind did tell mi yuh cumin" (I thought you were coming) she responded.

This was my first trip back home since I had left two years earlier. My parents and other relatives were delighted to have me home, but I had trouble readjusting. I found the nights too hot and could hardly sleep. I spent my nights sleeping on the floor as I searched for a cool spot.

I relished the Jamaican food and delicacies. Jamaican patties, jerked pork and chicken, sorrel, and cake were delicacies I had not had in ages. I thought I would "nyam till mi belly buss" (go into a gluttonous rave) but realized that I could only eat so much food in a day. Nonetheless, visiting all my relatives and friends and being fed delicious Jamaican food at every turn was a positive in my book.

I was able to sit with my parents and friends like old times even for that short visit. I was rejuvenated.

20
Emancipation

As I progressed on the journey from being an international graduate student to becoming a scholar, I realized that I entered the environment from a country with a rich colonial history steeped in hegemony that had Anglicized my worldview. These viewpoints fostered expectations and assumptions about my culture and other cultures globally. I accepted and realized that I was in a new community and did not particularly feel that I fit in. Along the way, I also understood that my experiences as a student here and in my host country differed significantly, and the cultural ethos of the university and its surrounding community was not similar to that with which I had become accustomed. Further, it was exasperated by my lack of cultural, social, and sometimes economic capital, which would have increased my chances of gaining a sense of belonging here.

As a learner, I understood that learning is transformational and that if I were to change, I had to take responsibility for my education and journey in the university. I needed to anticipate my role as a scholar and educator to assist others in finding their ways. Fundamentally, I had to engage the community in which I found myself and through situated learning move inward from being a peripheral learner through my earned capital. This recognition and the motivation I had to accomplish my goal of successful completion of my graduate studies helped me to reflect on my role as a student and individual critically.

Being lost in the struggles of daily life, I then recognized I was mostly on the peripheries of the learning environment or the edge of the academic community and needed to take action to "fend for myself." Recognizing my outsider status and my intended outcome of becoming a better scholar, I critically assessed my situation and reached inward to find strength, resolve, and agency to overcome these challenges. Thus, I needed to critically evaluate myself through a series of deep probes surrounding my personal histories, beliefs, and how these possibly affected my journey as an international student.

I knew that if I were to become an insider, I needed to participate in the academic, cultural, and social activities within the new environment. Participation in these activities would provide me with the requisite knowledge, skills, sensitivities, and behaviours that would allow me to function as a member of the group. For me, acquiring these skills was difficult, because I had entered the community of practice already acculturated in my Jamaican culture and ethnic behaviours. However, through a multilayered practice of observing, listening, speaking, reading, and writing, I became engaged in self-praxis because I needed to take ownership of my life and its trajectory. With that in mind, I became an active participant in my learning, and through this, I began to strengthen and interweave strands of language, literacy, and content learning.

I knew I was on the way to becoming a scholar when I understood that the academic directions of the university were poles apart from that to which I had become accustomed. This recognition and the motivation I had to accomplish my goal of successful completion of my graduate studies helped me to critically reflect on my role as a student and individual. From this process of contemplation, I was able to look past the issues I perceived and encountered.

Finding my voice through doing and redoing, observing how other classmates interpret text, solving problems, and synthesizing ideas for essays nudged me to develop agency and praxis, allowing me to take control of my life and progress from struggling to improving. As I reflected on my experiences, I realized that I became stronger by becoming more participatory in academic discussions as I learned increasingly challenging concepts and developed the language abilities to act accordingly. I realized that which caused me to bounce back came through my religious beliefs.

21
Overcoming

Christianity plays a central role in my life. A fundamental part of my youth was attending weekly Sunday church services and Sunday school. From these obligatory meetings I learned, developed, and to this day maintain strong Christian virtues, values, and morals; we learned unconditional love, kindness, hospitality, courtesy, patience, and loyalty. These continue to be the hallmark of my everyday existence. My strong Christian upbringing and conviction guide me in everything I do. These convictions were significant in my life as an international student.

Often, I reflect on my last Sunday in Jamaica. I attended church as usual. The message that day was particularly compelling. The deacon preached on 1 Kings 17:2–16. In this portion of scripture God provided supernaturally for Elijah, His servant after commanding him:

3 "Leave here, turn eastward and hide in the Kerith Ravine, east of the Jordan. **4** You will drink from the brook, and I have directed the ravens to supply you with food there."

I lived by the mantra that God would not take me this far to forsake me. Hence, I knew that whatever my struggles, it would all be well.

As I reflect on my journey as an international student, I have realized that my Christian belief and upbringing provided me the strength I needed to be resilient in the challenging situations I faced in my academic sojourn. I have always believed and depended upon, in absolute faith, a higher, infinite source as my guide. This belief always gave me hope, even in the face of life's most significant challenges. I somehow always knew beyond the shadow of a doubt that everything would be well on the other side of the problem. My faith in God never waned, and it allowed me to overcome the challenges I faced daily on my academic path.

Being a Christian enabled me to re-engage my spiritual side and accomplish calm faith and hope for a better future through turmoil. My Christian belief is grounded in three major concepts: faith, hope, and love. Hope and faith are two of the three characteristics that the apostle

Paul urged that all people should develop (1 Corinthians 13:13) to get them through life and its challenges. The third tenet is love, which Paul indicated is the most important character trait to have.

These tenets guided and still guides my path. So, I got involved in church activities. I never missed a Sunday service. I needed to stay connected to God and the community of believers. He is my peace, and by being in tune with Him, my faith developed and increased. I had hope in the future and that everything would work out for my good. Lastly, I was able to show and share the love with all I met. The love pouring out from me drew many international students to my side. Many confided in me, and I was able to offer advice and help many along their journeys. As a matter of fact, because of this love, I provided my services as a writing coach to many international students, free of charge.

Given my circumstances as a student, I would not have been able to accomplish as much as I did had I not leaned into God and relied on Him for strength. Therefore, in addition to the tenets of faith, hope, and love, prayer has been my lifeline. The prayers of my grandmother, mother, friends and fellow congregants at church both in Canada and Jamaica, gave me strength and the willpower to survive, despite the odds. The more I struggled, the harder I prayed, and the stronger my resolve became.

While preparing to defend my dissertation and faced an awkward situation, my only solace was to cry out to God.

After years of researching and writing, writing and rewriting, sending my final thesis back and forth, I was given the green light that I was ready to defend. I was preparing myself for defence. I had the urging to visit the graduate student office to deliver a hard copy of my thesis and inquire of the process and what next to do. I was hit with a bombshell! The process had stalled. They had halted the process because a member of the committee thought I should not be allowed to defend. This member, during the process, was away for much of the time and never attended a meeting or responded to emails. In her absence, the committee met several times. Once she responded to an email from the committee. Her response was that the committee should go ahead with the planned meetings and she would stand by the group's decision. What surprised me was that she never responded to the emails with the detailed description of the study's progress and committee decision.

Based on these deliberations, the committee decided that the study and process was at the point to be defended. They sent out the call for an external assessor and had acquired the services of one such person, who was interested in the work. After all this, with not a word to the committee expressing any sentiments, the absent professor wrote to the College of Graduate Studies, insisting that the defence be cancelled. In her words, I was "being ushered into a dissertation." Wow! How did I offend this person? She certainly had it in for me.

Hearing the news unsettled me. I felt betrayed. I emailed my supervisors to ask whether they knew about this. They were as shocked as I. The committee member had not bothered to inform them. Everyone was now in a tizzy as they tried to capture what had happened and what the next moves were to be. I was shattered. After all, I had worked so long and so hard, and now this obstacle was presented to me. That night, feeling weak and abandoned, I fell on my knees and cried and cried. Amidst my crying, I cried out to God.

"Lord, why me? I have done everything I should. I have worked on this project for so long. This person has never been to any of the recent meetings. She turned her rights over to the committee. Why now, Lord? Why me? Why me? Why me? Lord, help me. Lord, help me. Help me, Lord. Amen."

That was my plea as I cried out to God over and over that night. As I cried, I felt a peace come over me. I dried my tears and went to bed. As I slept, I had the assurance that He heard my cries and had answered. The next morning, I felt better and was able to deal with the situation that I had faced. I knew what to do.

I got up very early. I crafted a letter, to whom, I did not know. In my letter, I poured my heart out. I told the whole story and explained why I thought the move was unfair to me as a student. I had no idea what to do with the letter. I made some inquiries and learned that the letter should be directed to the Dean and Associate Dean of Graduate Studies.

I edited the letter and sent it to the relevant individuals by email. Shortly after that, I received a response that my case was being investigated. Within a day, they had reached a decision, and I could defend my thesis, as planned. In a letter, the College of Graduate Study apologized and wanted to know whether I wanted the case investigated further, because it was now a legal matter. I declined. All I wanted was to defend my hard work.

22
No Giving Up

Giving up is never an option for me. When I set a goal, I do what it takes to accomplish that goal. I act in faith to the completion of my task. Years ago, in my capacity as youth director of my church youth group, I planned a camp and retreat for young people in the churches. The venue was a place called River's Edge. River's Edge turned out to be an unusual name for an exciting destination. Unlike the journey to this place, River's Edge is a beautiful, rustic, laid-back group of cottages on a rural river bank in St. Mary, Jamaica. The river running through the property is gorgeous, serene, and calming. One naturally felt at peace at River's Edge.

Contrary to the place itself, the journey to River's Edge was long, lonely, winding, and rugged. The terrain and bumpy roads caused the vehicles to bump much like the bounce-about at the Six Flags Amusement Park. The treacherous stretches of road on the rickety bridge threatened to drop our bus into the deep below. There were groans, screams, and vehement requests to quit the journey and go home. We nearly did.

Then the bus pulled into a driveway, and there was a hush from the young congregants. Mouths gaped and eyes fixed on the paradise before them. Someone shouted, "This is heaven!" In the Bible, the road to heaven is described as narrow, much like the one we had just travelled to get to this place.

My progression through international studentship reminded me of my journey to River's Edge. As I reflected on being a student, I realized that there had been many bumps along the road for me, mostly due to my lack of social, academic, cultural and sometimes linguistic capital. The failed attempts, the writer's block I often nervously faced, and the many things I lacked remind me of my journey to that majestic location in rural Jamaica. There are considerable differences between the formality of the Jamaican education system and the looser but academically rigorous university culture and its local, provincial community of practice. During my studies, I was often stuck in my head; my views, steeped in hegemonic practices and Euro-centricity, and I needed to experience a paradigm shift. I had to extend myself to see that which remained hidden more clearly.

Like others before me and many to come, I did not particularly feel that I fit into this environment. My path and intentions were clear. I was determined that I would complete my course of study successfully. As a learner, I understood that learning was transformational and to be transformed, and I had to take responsibility for my learning and anticipate my role as a researcher, scholar, and educator to assist others in finding their way. Principally, I had to engage the communities of practice in which I found myself, and through situated learning and triple learning move inward, from being a learner always on the periphery, into academia through my earned capital. This negotiation in many ways has been the nucleus of this book.

While conversing and decoding conversations I had with colleagues and other international students, I became aware that I did not fit in due to my skewed perspective on learning and academia. These conversations helped me come to terms with the fact that I had entered my program with my ideas about life and study overseas. Their comments, stories, and questions helped me face how deeply steeped I had become in the revolving hegemony of my Jamaican education, and to see that I needed to approach my studies and life overseas from a broader, more reflective and analytic framework. The predominant hegemonic practices had failed me. I had hoped for a linear progression of both my life and study. In reality, the process was nonlinear, and that resulted in my feeling of alienation.

Throughout the process I cried, I screamed, I joked, I sang, and then I cried again. "Lord tek di case and gimmi di pilla" (Lord help me! I cannot handle this). Had it been up to me and my strength, perhaps I would have yielded to the voice that said, "What are you doing? Who said you could do this? This journey is too difficult." But I had a Friend who walked with me. We talked along the way, and He assured me that He was with me; I just needed to continue the path.

So, like the river that never flows backward, I sustained my forward path, embracing my resilience and strength in God. I ignored the voices of negativity and surrounded myself with calming and positive vibes. "You can do it. Yes, you can. Just keep at it. You will be fine, dear." Determined to make it to the end, I engaged my community of practice and through situated learning moved inward from the periphery through my earned capital. And like our bus driver, who shifted and turned as he negotiated the rugged terrain of the country road to find new paths that would take us to River's Edge, I persisted.

I continually envisioned the light at the end of the tunnel. As I got closer, the stories became more evident, the burdens got lighter, and the thoughts began to flow more freely. As my thoughts flew in every direction, I was able to understand my journey as an international graduate student. As I grew to appreciate the ethos of the institution, my conversations, and interactions with local and international students as well as the facilities within the university that continually left me with mixed feelings. I regularly wrestled with the nature of international studentship. Through the development of my critical thinking skills, I was able to look at the broad picture of being an international student and contemplate my circumstance in a way that allowed me to look at this phenomenon differently.

Finally, I was empowered. I, myself, have walked the path to becoming a scholar. I was transformed; I had become a scholar; I have evolved. I continue to grow, to become. I consequently learned to acknowledge that I am in a new space, one with which I was very much unfamiliar. I needed to accept this unfamiliarity for what it was and be respectful of this unique place and ways of being and doing. When I acknowledged, accepted, and became respectful of the change in the landscape, I was able to bloom into the flower I was meant to be. I completed my doctoral thesis successfully.

I am sometimes still torn between "there" and "here": my country of origin, Jamaica, and Canada, my country of temporary settlement. I wandered between the two worlds because I nostalgically dream of my homeland with the hope of someday returning and rebuilding a life there. Yet, I lived and was obligated to fit into Canadian culture and lifestyle. I am always conscious of my outsider position; this keeps me grounded and focused on being successful. It was not an easy road, but through participation, praxis, and practice it got easier as the days progressed. Like Robert Frost wrote, "I took the one less travelled by, and that has made all the difference."

God favoured me in the process. The very thesis that was deemed unfit, that year won the Social Sciences B award campus-wide. I presented a stellar defence, and the external assessor nominated my thesis for this award. The award was to reward excellence and originality in a graduate research paper. Had I not been persistent in calling out to God, perhaps I would still not have defended my thesis.

23
Success at Last

Fast forward four and a half years. I stood on the cusp of change. I was conferred with a Doctor of Philosophy degree (PhD) in Interdisciplinary Studies. In the audience, among the sea of faces, was a small group of friends who had become like family. They were there as my support, my cheerleaders. This moment had been a long time coming, and they were happy to witness this great accomplishment.

Funny how they call it a terminal degree! My journey had been long and hard, but it had culminated well. Indeed, I was made to be the head and not the tail, because at the end of it all my dissertation was awarded the best thesis of the term. There was also a cash reward attached to the award.

As I entered the auditorium backstage, there was great excitement among the graduating class. There were members of staff on hand to assist us in finding our places. As I searched for my group and the assigned area, a woman from the college of graduate studies approached me.

"Congratulations Yolanda!" she said. "I noticed your feature on the graduate student website."

"Thank you," I replied. I had seen the feature just minutes before and thought it was well done.

"Can we have a picture of you in your gown?"

"Sure," I said.

"Thank you," she responded taking my program and pointing me to an area before the college poster. I smiled, and the camera flashed. Moving on, I met and greeted other graduates, some of whom I knew, others I did not. In all the rush and bustle backstage, we lost track of time. The music started, and we began to move. Coming around the corner, we were greeted by faculty members applauding and smiling. They had formed a line along the hallway as we entered the auditorium through a side door accessible from the back, where moments before we were preparing for this moment. I, along with the over two hundred other graduates, marched past, smiling and feeling proud. We entered the auditorium and sat in order.

As I stood in line, waiting to cross the stage, my years as a student flashed before my eyes. So much has happened since September 2011. I fought back the tears as I considered my life to this point. I had transitioned from my very humble beginnings to the grandest stage of all. Had I not been strong, I would not have made it. It took guts and grit to have come this far.

Wearing my academic regalia of black, green, and yellow, I looked stunning. I was elated to be adorned so fittingly. These colours already bore significance to me because they were the colours of our beloved Jamaican flag. I sat in the sea of graduates as one by one the names were called, from undergraduate to graduate students. I stood proudly, decked in the colours of our beloved Jamaica. These colours now bore new significance, as that day, wearing those colours, I was to be conferred a Doctor of Philosophy. I stood proud and strong. I had made it! I had overcome.

As the announcer prepared to call my name, I stood erect and marched on to collect my parchment from the university's head. As my name sounded over the speakers, "Yolanda Michelle Palmer," I proudly tossed my tassel to the left and boldly stepped across the stage, into the proverbial fold. Walking across the stage was a very proud moment for me, my relatives back home in Jamaica, who were watching online, and the few friends scattered in the audience who cheered loudly, expressing their pride and joy in my accomplishment. Among these few friends seated in the auditorium was that special someone who had, in the latter years of my study, crept into my life and had stolen my heart.

Greeted by my beaming supervisor and mentor, I was escorted to join the community of scholars on the podium. All eyes on me, literally, as the spotlights gleamed. The journey, at least this portion of it, has ended. I am now a member of the academic community.

24
Finding a Job

Gaining employment after a PhD can be an overwhelming experience. After spending years researching, studying, and writing, one would naturally hope to be among the twenty-five percent who gain employment in their field of study, and even more so, in the upper echelon of the working society. Very often, life after the terminal degree does not follow that pattern. Things do not happen overnight; instead there is a gradual process. The process for everyone is different. What is sure is that each must pay his or her dues to society in some way.

In my case, it took a few attempts. I applied for countless jobs to no avail. In a few cases, I was called into the offices of directors only to be informed that I was overqualified for these positions. I applied for a job I know I was qualified for, and was called into the office of the director who bluntly told me (ignoring my qualifications altogether) that I was unqualified. I was *not qualified*, he said. I could understand if he said I needed the currency of the area, but to say I am unqualified I thought was quite demeaning and belittling. At times, I felt like I was writing for a degree in job searching. Another PhD!

To survive, I took odd jobs. The first real job I had after leaving the university was a clerical post. I was keeping inventory. While doing this, I was still writing my degree in job applications. Nothing seemed to be forthcoming. I knew there was a greater plan for my life, a higher calling, and so I continued to scout the employment sites and pages for job opportunities.

I started receiving short-term contractual work. Among my many precarious positions, I have been a Research Assistant, Research Coordinator, Sessional Lecturer, Graduate Student Coordinator. These positions kept me going. As I did these jobs, I continued to apply and hope for more permanent posts, which seemed few and far between.

These days, I enjoy being the instructor of students who walk the paths I have walked; international students who want to enter programs of study at university. I currently work with graduate and undergraduate international students with English as a second language helping them by preparing them for and facilitating their transition into university. Given my background as an international student, researcher, and educator, I see many students enter classrooms like this term after term, not having the requisite literacy skills to function in the university fully. I hear their questions; I feel their frustrations and understand their situations all too well. Even with my English background, I also was severely challenged in the university. I love my job and thoroughly enjoy working with these students, being fully aware of their struggles.

25
New Beginnings

I sat at my desk awaiting the arrival of my newest batch of students on the first day of term. Caught in a reverie, my mind wandered to a time seven years ago when I, like these eager, ambitious, yet tentative students became an international student. My mind flashed to my first day as an international student and the contrasting feelings I had as I entered my very first class, the many processes I engaged as I learned the ways of the university, challenges I successfully negotiated, and the many seasons I endured.

It was a cold winter day with temperatures dipping way below zero. It was the kind of day on which the cold seeps deep into your bones, through every layer and into the soles of your feet. The trees were all white and beautifully decorated with hoarfrost, forming an icy forest. In the background, hidden behind clear blue skies, stood the sun. This was the kind of stuff you see captured on postcards labelled "Greetings from across the miles." Thankfully, I was inside where it was warm. I hate being out in the cold.

As the new students filed in, clothed in large winter jackets, their reddened cheeks told an all too familiar story. Their dripping boots left puddles along the tiled surfaces; giving further evidence of the path they had trod to get here. Watching them stream in, my line of consciousness zoomed in, realizing that each one is reminiscent of my own story; a story of wandering and wondering, of one who has left native lands to traverse unfamiliar destinies. Their stories mirrored mine. I too was as they are. I too have traversed the cold and prayed for the moment I could come in from the cold.

I could sense the questions in their eyes, masked by the shy smiles as they approached my desk for the first time. They greeted each other; some heartily; others shyly. I watched in awe as I saw a story mirrored in each face. As I watched them enter the classroom, I could not help remembering. I could not help wondering what their stories were. What made them leave their homelands to study overseas?

I wondered how these new students, who had travelled across oceans to study here, were faring with these frigid temperatures. The weather, like the academic and social environment, was an unfamiliar terrain that newcomers would most definitely need to traverse and conquer to achieve their social and academic goals successfully. They were coming into the cold, literally and figuratively.

When one has been in the cold, one understands and appreciates the joy and relief that comes when one can come in from the cold. *Coming in from the cold* symbolically means the individual has become accepted or recognized, especially by a group of people like domestic students and professors. In keeping with my culture, my mind flashed to the famous song written and performed by Bob Marley, "Coming in from the Cold."

Coming in from the cold, admittedly, is way more engaging and exciting than being in the cold. As the students entered, I smiled and greeted each one, inquiring about their wellbeing. Welcome! Come in from the cold.

A word of advice

The opportunity to study overseas is an exciting stage of life. The journey is filled with many opportunities and challenges. You, like so many others before you, have what it takes to complete this journey successfully. You too can come in from the cold.

As you move into your academic sojourn, know that you are fully capable of making this journey. It is a journey on which you will feel lonesome. Remember, within you lies the strength to complete the task. At times, you might be torn between here and your home country. Learn to accept the new environment. It is now your new home, at least for a while. Settle in well. Get involved in the community. Remember that at least for this short span you will have to live in this new environment. Get used to it!

Quit complaining! It does not help. Own your space in the arena. Be bold. Be confident. Be strong. God has not given you a spirit of fear but of power, and love, and a sound mind.

There are several ways to demonstrate resilience and be successful in one's academic dreams overseas. One can do so through self-determination, relationships and networks, engagement in clubs and societies, spirituality, culture, specialized programs and courses, and support systems at the university.

Be confident in your knowledge. Own it and defend it with all you have. Only seek to strengthen your arguments with research. No one knows your story better than you do. I caution you here also to be humble. Arrogance is a defeater in an unknown space. With humility, confidently own your space and your story.

Build and maintain strong relationships. Having strong relationships will help you to overcome or bounce back from challenges. These relationships may be with domestic, other international students, family members, and professors.

Get involved in clubs and societies. These organizations help to promote friendships among international students and peers. Many international students find support in the stories of others, through these clubs and societies for international students going through adverse situations, which help them adjust successfully into the new culture.

If you are a spiritual person, stay grounded in God. During troubled times, faith in God allows you to overcome the challenges faced daily on your academic path.

Engage and participate in cultural activities. Many have found comfort and strength in participating in the culture of their homelands. Language, food, dress, religion, and games are significant cultural resources that serve as protective factors against stress and challenges.

Take advantage of and participate in specific programs and courses arranged by your university, colleges, and departments to help you reach optimal academic performance and be able to engage in cultural exchanges within the academy responsibly. These courses and programs are specialized as they aim to assist you in overcoming specific problems. Many universities offer writing help and classes. These are very useful when entering programs of study overseas from a different academic culture.

Many universities have support systems in place for students coming from overseas. These programs are generally designed to help sojourner students, like you, become familiar with the services on campus. Find out where and what these are and get involved.

Learn to acknowledge, accept, and respect your new environment and its differences. Acknowledge that you are in a new place and things are different. Accept the differences between your home country and the host country. Respect the fact that you are in a new environment. When you acknowledge, accept, and respect these differences you are better able to move forward in your journey as an international student.

All in all, when in Rome, do as the Romans do. Be observant, be inquisitive, unlearn, learn, relearn. Model your actions from responsible domestic students and professors.

My friend once cautioned me that an international education

gives you the wings and pushes you off the cliff. You must learn how to fly. No one will teach you how to fly. It shows you how to be independent.

Independence comes through hard work, but you have the wherewithal to survive this journey and be successful.

Blessings and guidance,

Yolanda.

Works Cited

Angelou, M. (1969). I know why the caged bird sings. UK. Heinemann

Banton, Buju. "It's not an easy road." *Til Shiloh*, 1995. MP3.

Byrne, B. (2009), March 14. Let's make a prediction: The weather forecast will be right or wrong. Retrieved from https://www.therecord.com/opinion-story/2561689-let-s-make-a-prediction-the-weather-forecast-will-be-right-or-wrong/

Camus, A. (1988). *The stranger.* New York: Vintage International, Vintage Books.

Canadian Mental Health Association (n.d). Seasonal affective disorder. Retrieved from https://cmha.bc.ca/documents/seasonal-affective-disorder-2/

Connor, H. (2019, January 31). Lack of jobs leads CBU international students to soup kitchen. Retrieved from https://www.cbc.ca/news/canada/nova-scotia/lack-of-jobs-leads-cbu-international-students-to-soup-kitchen-1.4996266

Egbo, B. (2008). *Teaching for diversity in Canadian schools.* Toronto: Pearson.

Finnerman, W., Tisch, S., Starkey, S., & Newirth, C. (Producers) & Zemeckis, R. (Director). (1994). Forrest Gump [Motion Picture]. USA: Paramount Pictures

hooks, b. (1988). Talking back. Toronto, Ontario: Between the Lines.

Merleau-Ponty, M. (2012). *Phenomenology of perception* (D. A. Landes, Trans.). London: Routledge.

Murray, D. M. (1985). *A writer teaches writing* (2nd ed.). Boston: Houghton Mifflin Co.

Villanueva Jr., V. (1993*). Bootstraps: From an American academic of color.* United States of America: National Council of Teachers of English.

Rodriguez, R. (1982). *Hunger of memory: The education of Richard Rodriguez.* New York: Bantam Books.

The Critical Thinking Community (2013). *Defining critical thinking.* Retrieved from http://www.criticalthinking.org/pages/defining-critical-thinking/766

CPSIA information can be obtained
at www.ICGtesting.com
Printed in the USA
LVHW020228021119
636120LV00003B/3/P